# **MINDSET** FOR THE **FUTURE**

**TRAVEL**

# *About the Authors*

Bridgette Di Ferdinando

Bridgette is an award-winning Social Psychologist, lifelong nomad and expert in Culture and behavior transformation. She has spent over 20 years in global executive and advisory roles, working with governments, corporations and the arts on shifting mindsets to lead, grow and collaborate in challenging environments. Bridgette has travelled the globe to collaborate and author research, invent technologies, and introduce ancient wisdoms in her work on behavior, with the aim of bringing diverse groups, leaders and cultures together, for the better. She calls both Brisbane and Barcelona home. This is her first book.

Sacha Cornuault

Sacha is a researcher, writer, and consultant whose work sits at the intersection of neuroscience, leadership, and human development. His first book, Teach the Brain, examines how students and educators learn, adapt, and perform in complex environments. Over the past decade, Sacha has worked across business and leadership development, and for the past three years he has focused specifically on applied neuroscience, helping executives and organizations translate cognitive science into practical tools for change. Originally from France and now based in Australia, Sacha brings a lived understanding of mobility, identity, and cultural transition that shapes both his research and his writing. His work on this book draws together his long-standing interest in neuroscience, his experience of migration, and his fascination with how travel shapes human behavior.

# **MINDSET** FOR THE **FUTURE**

**TRAVEL**

BRIDGETTE M. B. DI FERDINANDO
SACHA S. G. CORNUAULT

Copyright © 2025 by Mindset Publishing LLC. All rights reserved.

No part of this book may be copied, reproduced, stored, distributed, or transmitted in any form - electronic, mechanical, photocopying, recording, or otherwise without prior written permission from the author or publisher, except as permitted by applicable copyright law. Unauthorized reproduction, distribution, or resale of this book, in whole or in part, is strictly prohibited and may result in legal action.

Every effort has been made to ensure the accuracy, completeness, and relevance of the information presented in this book. However, the author and publisher make no guarantees or warranties, express or implied, regarding its applicability to individual circumstances. The content is provided 'as is' for informational and educational purposes only. The author and publisher disclaim any liability for any loss, damage, or consequences resulting from the use or interpretation of this material. The views and opinions expressed in this book are those of the authors and do not represent the perspectives of any organization.

Professional & Ethical Disclaimer: This book is intended to provoke reflection and discussion about travel, identity, and human development. It does not constitute psychological, legal, medical, or business advice. The insights presented are based on research, lived experience, and professional knowledge, but should not replace guidance from qualified professionals in specific fields. Readers are encouraged to consider context and consult appropriate experts when applying ideas from this book in personal or professional practice. The author and publisher assume no responsibility for decisions made based on the contents of this work.

Title: Mindset for the Future: Travel

Authors: Bridgette Di Ferdinando and Sacha S. G. Cornuault

Publisher: Mindset Publishing LLC

Subject: Travel | Psychology | Culture | Human Development

Cover Design by Claire Woodfield

Illustrations by: Bridgette Di Ferdinando and Sacha S. G. Cornuault

ISBN (Paperback): 978-1-7640093-7-9 | For permission or enquiries, contact: mindsetpublishingllc@gmail.com

For all who have supported me, and pushed me to (finally) put a book out there on a topic that I'm so passionate about, travel, using everything I know about the human mind - you know who you are. I'm forever grateful for your wisdom and insights. And to my son, Leonardo. Watching you absorb life's experiences with wonder and incorporate them in your growth has been my greatest inspiration. This book is for you. - *Bridgette*

To my parents, grandparents, Emma, Mickael and Julianna, your support has shaped every part of this journey. For those who have not yet experienced the freedom of travel, may this work encourage you to explore. To my little cherry, thank you for being a quiet source of light along the way. - *Sacha*

"Wherever my travels may lead, paradise is where I am."

*- Voltaire*

# Contents

| | |
|---|---|
| Introduction | 1 |
| PART 1 - The Meaning of Travel is Changing | 6 |
|   Why We Travel | 10 |
|   Travel as Identity | 16 |
|   Identity Reinvention | 25 |
|   The Death of the Bucket List | 28 |
|   The Value of Intentional Travel | 35 |
|   Regenerative Travel | 40 |
|   Travel as Privilege | 44 |
| PART 2 - The Mind on The Move | 49 |
|   Discomfort as Growth | 53 |
|   Attention in New Environments | 61 |
|   The Neuroscience of Awe | 67 |
|   Memory, Place and Meaning | 74 |
|   Stillness & Retreat | 80 |
|   Micro-Exploration | 83 |
| PART 3 - The New Rules of Exploration | 88 |
|   Digital Nomads and Remote Realities | 92 |

| | |
|---|---|
| AI Itineraries, Human Choice | 98 |
| Connection, Intensity and the Shared Journey | 104 |
| Language, Culture and Humility | 110 |
| The Psychology of Belonging Abroad. | 116 |
| Travel and Power | 120 |
| | |
| PART 4 - Becoming a Conscious Explorer | 125 |
| The Mindset of Listening | 128 |
| Coming Home Changed | 134 |
| Travel as a State of Mind | 139 |
| Travel and Well-being | 144 |
| The Loneliness & Connection Paradox | 149 |
| Intercultural Competence | 154 |
| The Role of Storytelling | 158 |
| | |
| PART 5 - Considerations | 162 |
| Considerations for the Traveler | 166 |
| Considerations for the Travel Industry | 172 |
| Considerations for Corporate Explorers | 179 |
| Travel in Times of Crisis | 185 |
| Where is Travel Going Next? | 189 |
| Conclusion | 196 |
| A Traveler's Toolkit | 199 |
| References | 208 |

# Introduction

This book examines how movement shapes the way we think, learn, and relate to the world. Travel influences our assumptions, attention, and behavior, and these shifts matter in a time of rapid global change.

*Mindset for the Future: Travel* looks at how travel intersects with identity, cognition, technology and adaptation. It draws on neuroscience, psychology and global mobility research while also offering practical guidance for today's travelers, whether they are exploring for personal growth, working across cultures, or designing travel experiences for others.

Throughout the book, the writing style combines philosophical reflections, practical tips and relevant cognitive science to show how movement affects mindset. When we talk about travel in this book, it is not limited to holidays or leisure. It considers travel in all its forms, from short trips to long-term mobility, including the experiences of corporate travelers, digital nomads and individuals moving between cultures. It asks how travel can help us understand ourselves and others, and how we might approach it with more curiosity, responsibility and intention.

The way we move through the world is shaping how we think. Every border we cross, cultural; geographic; and digital, presses on our existing assumptions, changes what we believe and realigns what we notice. Travel builds awareness. It sharpens attention, disrupts routine, builds new routines, and reveals what often goes unnoticed in familiar settings. In a time of rapid change, these shifts in perception matter. They affect how we learn, lead, connect, and make decisions.

Today, travel functions as a way for people to learn about and strive to understand other cultures, one that extends beyond itineraries and passports. The ability to travel consciously is increasingly linked to self-awareness, cultural humility, ecological responsibility, and psychological agility. The return on investment for this form of travel is not measured in miles but in perspective, resilience, and relational depth, capacities that define modern leadership, global citizenship, and emotional intelligence. As travel becomes more curated, comfortable, and commodified, this book invites us to approach movement as a discipline, one that cultivates inner expansion and empowers us to leave places, relationships, and communities better than we found them, rather than treating it as just consumption.

Shared experiences, whether with family, friends, colleagues, or fellow seekers sit at the heart of this evolution. Journeying alongside others challenges our assumptions, tests our empathy, and deepens our understanding in ways solitary travel cannot always achieve. The stories we build together become the foundation for connection, trust, and collective insight. Travel becomes not only personal transformation, but social transformation.

As modern travel increasingly prioritizes ease, efficiency, and curated experiences, we risk losing the resilience that once came from navigating the unfamiliar. Convenience can shield us from the very experiences that once expanded our courage, creativity, and adaptability. A future-ready travel mindset asks us to step beyond curated certainty and rekindle our willingness to encounter the unknown, to risk surprise, dialogue, and even discomfort in service of growth.

Considerations for the reader
As you enter this book, consider how movement through travel, whether a big trip or weekend away, has shaped who you are. Ask:
- Do I travel to consume or to transform?
- How do I measure the value of a journey?
- When do I embrace uncertainty when I travel, and when do I avoid it?
- Do I leave places and people better from my presence?
- Who do I become when I move alongside others?

These are not only travel questions, they are life questions. Let them guide how you move through the pages ahead.

# PART 1

# The Meaning of Travel is Changing

"Not all who wander are lost."

*J.R.R Tolkien*

## THE MEANING OF TRAVEL IS CHANGING

Why do we travel? In the past, it may have been a question answered with simplicity: to rest, to escape, to discover a permanent or temporary place to call home. Or to satisfy a curiosity about an external reference point; a culture, a country or specific destination. But in a world increasingly shaped by global mobility, digital identity, and shifting cultural values, the reasons we move and what we seek when we do are more layered than ever. This section examines the deeper forces behind our desire to explore, uncovering how the act of travel has evolved from a physical journey into a tool for psychological growth, identity formation and evolution, and future readiness.

In these opening chapters, we explore the human impulse to move, tracing it from our evolutionary roots and early migrations to the complex motivations that guide modern travelers. Through research in psychology, neuroscience, and sociology, we investigate why novelty stimulates the brain, how curiosity has driven cultural exchange, and why discomfort can serve as a catalyst for change. Travel, we argue, is more than a break from routine; it is one of the most powerful levers we have for mindset development and to establish new or realigned habits. We also examine the growing connection between travel and identity. In a globally connected world, being a traveler is often part of how individuals define themselves not just through where they've been, but through how they've changed as a result. Whether through digital storytelling, social media presence, or the pursuit of global citizenship, the traveler's narrative is becoming a public artifact of personal evolution. This raises important questions: Is travel still about place, or has it become a projection of self? Can it still offer transformation when commodified? Finally, we challenge the conventional "bucket list" approach to travel, a model rooted in acquisition, volume, social validation and perceived societal status. As global realities shift due to climate, access, and digital saturation, we propose a different framework: one that prioritizes presence over performance, intention over itinerary. We explore how travel can move from a transactional checklist often set by others to a self-transformational practice; one aligned with values, relationships, and adaptability.

In Part 1, readers are invited to examine their own reasons for traveling, to confront the assumptions embedded in modern tourism, and to open themselves to a richer, more meaningful relationship with movement. Travel is changing, not just in where we go, but in why we go. Understanding this shift is the first step toward developing a mindset prepared for a world where mobility, identity, and connection are increasingly fluid. This mindset is becoming not only personally meaningful but strategically important. Travelers who cultivate curiosity, emotional intelligence, cultural literacy, and presence gain returns far beyond memories and enjoyment. The return on investment of conscious travel appears in adaptability, creativity, resilience, leadership capacity, and relational depth. In a world where attention and perspective are competitive advantages, those who travel with intention are better equipped to navigate uncertainty, collaborate across cultures, and contribute thoughtfully to a shared global future.

# Why We Travel

Movement is part of who we are. Long before air travel, before maps, even before written language, humans were in motion. Across deserts and mountains, across oceans and generations, we moved. Sometimes by necessity, searching for food, fleeing danger, chasing the seasons. Sometimes by instinct, pushed forward by a restlessness that no village or border could contain. Travel, in its earliest form, was about survival. But even then, there was something more. Something harder to explain, yet unmistakably human: a deep, internal pull toward the unknown.

## THE MEANING OF TRAVEL IS CHANGING

Today, we travel for a range of different reasons. For leisure; learning; and the thrill of stepping into someplace unfamiliar. We build itineraries, take photos, seek experiences, but underneath the convenience of modern transport lies the same age-old impulse to explore, grow and expand the boundaries of what we know. Travel, in this sense, is more than movement through space; it is movement through perception, identity, and understanding. To grasp why we travel, we must first look to our evolutionary past.

From a biological standpoint, the drive to explore new territory once increased our chances of survival. Evolutionary psychologists have suggested that humans evolved to balance two competing tendencies: neophobia, the fear of new things and neophilia, the attraction to them. While too much risk could be fatal, some level of novelty-seeking offered advantages: new food sources, better shelter, new mates, and more secure terrain. Those willing to venture beyond the familiar sometimes found what they needed to survive and eventually, to thrive. This balance still exists in us today.

Though our environments have changed, our brains have not evolved much since the Paleolithic era.

The same circuits that once evaluated whether a new valley was worth entering now help us decide whether to book a flight to another continent, switch careers, or immerse ourselves in a foreign culture. We are still wired to assess, explore, and learn from what lies beyond the edge of our comfort zones. This idea of seeking beyond the known is also embedded in our psychological development.

Maslow's hierarchy of needs, one of the most enduring frameworks in human motivation, places self-actualization, the pursuit of growth, meaning, and purpose at the top of human aspiration. Once basic needs are met, people often seek experiences that allow them to expand emotionally and intellectually. Travel, when done with intention, satisfies this need. It offers new perspectives, demands adaptability, and fosters connection. It feeds not only our curiosity but also our desire to become more fully ourselves. As travel has become safer and more accessible to far more people than ever before, its meaning has shifted in many cases. In ancient times, journeys were often tied to pilgrimage, a physical movement that mirrored a spiritual one. From the Camino de Santiago to the Hajj, these sacred paths emphasized humility, reflection, a reminder of one's place in nature and transformation. The journey was the lesson, and hardship was not avoided but embraced.

In contrast, much of today's travel industry emphasizes comfort and consumption. Destinations are marketed, experiences are compressed and packaged, and efficiency is prized. Yet even within this modern landscape, the deeper motivations persist. People still crave meaning, and seek to evolve.

Sociologically, travel has also been a way to explore identity. In the 19th and early 20th centuries, the "Grand Tour" was seen as a rite of passage for Europe's elite, a way for young men (and eventually women) to cultivate sophistication through exposure to art, language, and culture. Today, travel continues to shape how we see ourselves and how we wish to be seen. Whether it's a gap year, a sabbatical, or a solo backpacking trip, travel serves as a narrative device, a way to rewrite or rediscover our story. This is particularly relevant in the age of social media, where our experiences are shared and curated for public consumption. Travel becomes a form of self-expression, a statement of values, aspirations, and belonging. But travel also serves cognitive and emotional functions that go beyond identity.

Neurologically, novelty stimulates the brain's reward centers, releasing dopamine and increasing engagement. New environments, experiences or spontaneous and unexpected experiences challenge our habits, interrupt autopilot thinking, and force us to be more aware. We pay closer attention, listen more carefully and become present. In many ways, travel provides a neurological reset, one that allows us to break patterns and reconnect with a sense of wonder often dulled by routine. This sense of wonder, some call wanderlust, is both a feeling and a function. It's not a desire to escape, but a yearning to learn, to grow, to encounter the world in ways that stretch our thinking. Research into "awe" and "cognitive flexibility" suggests that exposure to vast, unfamiliar, or beautiful experiences expands our mental models. We become less rigid, more open, and better equipped to handle complexity.

This is the real value of travel in the modern age: not just as entertainment, but as education. However, it's worth asking: is all travel inherently meaningful? The answer, of course, is no. Movement alone doesn't guarantee growth. For travel to be transformative, it requires intention, reflection, and presence. It demands that we approach the unfamiliar not just as tourists, but as learners willing to be challenged, to be wrong, to be changed.

In the chapters that follow, we'll explore how this shift in the meaning of travel is playing out in real time. We'll look at how travel shape's identity, how digital culture is reframing what it means to be a traveler, and why the model of bucket-list tourism no longer serves a world in flux. But before we move forward, this chapter offers a grounding truth: we travel because we are human. And to travel well in the future, we must first understand what has always moved us in the past.

Travel today also raises a new question: are we preserving the spirit of exploration, or numbing it? Modern travel culture often rewards convenience, predictability, and curated comfort. But when travel becomes too controlled, we risk weakening the very capacities movement was designed to strengthen; adaptability, improvisation, and courage. A future-ready travel mindset embraces calculated risk and gentle discomfort not as inconvenience, but as a training ground. If we insulate ourselves from uncertainty, we also insulate ourselves from growth.

# Travel as Identity

Crossing into unfamiliar places can reveal unexpected parts of ourselves. Away from the habits, roles, and reference points of daily life, identity becomes more visible, both in what changes and in what remains. For many, travel offers moments of contrast that clarify how they see themselves, where they feel belonging, and what stories they carry. In a world shaped by movement and visibility, those moments increasingly influence how people express who they are.

## THE MEANING OF TRAVEL IS CHANGING

This chapter explores the relationship between travel and identity not as a status symbol or rite of passage, but as one of many ways people reflect on selfhood, culture, and meaning. We look at how place and movement shape personal narrative, how exposure to difference impacts self-perception, and how, for some, travel becomes part of the language they use to explain who they've become.

Geography remains central to identity. Where we are born, where we live, and the cultural contexts we move through all shape how we understand ourselves and how others understand us. Historically, these ties were more rigid. Movement was rare, often risky, and those who traveled were seen as outsiders, traders, pilgrims, or wanderers. Today, those boundaries are more fluid. Technology allows us to see across continents, social platforms let us showcase our journeys in real time, and global exposure has become an aspirational marker of education, adaptability, and status. Travel has moved from the margins of life to the center of how many people express purpose, values, and curiosity.

This shift has deep psychological underpinnings. As demonstrated by the following narrative identity map, we understand ourselves through the stories we tell about our lives, where we've been, what we've overcome and how we've grown.

## NARRATIVE IDENTITY MAP

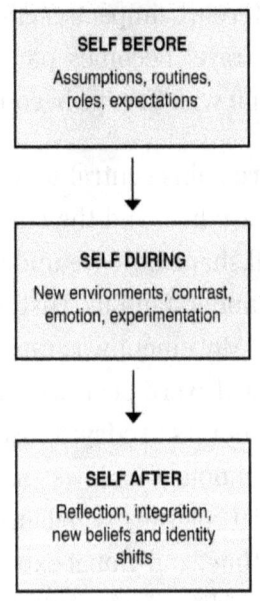

Travel naturally lends itself to this kind of narrative construction. Each trip becomes a chapter, each destination a metaphor. "The summer I went to Morocco," "When I lived in Berlin," "That trek through Patagonia", these stories are more than memories;

they are self-shaping tools. They help us refine and give coherence to how we see ourselves.

Travel also functions as a catalyst for identity exploration. Away from the routines and expectations of our home environments, we are given the rare opportunity to experiment. The anonymity of unfamiliar places can be liberating. Without the scripts of daily life, job titles, social circles, cultural norms, we have room to try on new ways of being. This can range from the subtle (a different rhythm of life, new foods, different styles of interaction) to the profound (rethinking values, reimagining goals, or rediscovering passion). In this way, travel offers not just a change in scenery, but a change in self-concept.

The brain is an integral part of this transformation. Novel environments activate the brain's attentional systems, prompting increased activity in the hippocampus, responsible for memory formation, and the prefrontal cortex, which governs decision-making and self-reflection. When we are immersed in new cultures we rely more on conscious cognitive processing rather than habitual responses. This state of heightened awareness enhances our ability to form new neural pathways, reinforcing the adaptability and flexibility central to identity evolution. Importantly, these environments also stimulate the production of dopamine, the neurotransmitter associated with reward and motivation, which supports engagement and learning in unfamiliar contexts. The identity-shaping potential of travel becomes even more visible in the digital age.

Social media platforms like Instagram, YouTube, and TikTok have transformed travel into a performative space, a way of signaling who we are, what we value, and how we want to be seen. The "traveler self" is now curated through photos, captions, vlogs, and stories. In this sense, travel is both an experience and a brand. It can reflect authentic growth, but it can also slip into performative consumption, travel as proof of freedom, sophistication, or success. This duality presents both opportunity and risk. On one hand, sharing our experiences can inspire others, build community, and invite deeper reflection. On the other hand, it can distort reality, reinforcing the idea that travel is only meaningful if it's dramatic, beautiful, or publicly visible. This creates a kind of pressure: not just to travel, but to be a traveler, someone with stories, images, and credentials that validate a certain kind of

lifestyle. In this environment, the boundary between genuine exploration and image crafting can become blurred. Yet beyond the filters and the photos, there remains a deeper truth: travel genuinely changes us.

When we immerse ourselves in other cultures, we confront differences, linguistic, social, religious, and political. We are exposed to new ways of thinking, different modes of being, and values that challenge our assumptions. These moments of friction when we feel confused, disoriented, or even uncomfortable are not signs of failure. They are the raw materials of growth. They allow us to question who we are and what we stand for, often in ways that would be impossible without the perspective that distance provides. Psychologically, these experiences often engage what developmental theorists call "identity moratorium" a period of exploration without commitment. This is essential to identity growth, particularly during transitions.

Beyond individual identity exploration, travel also creates a temporary but powerful form of social identity. When we step into the role of "traveler," we enter a loose, short-lived community, one bound not by nationality or background, but by movement, curiosity, and shared displacement. For a brief period, strangers become companions because we recognize ourselves in one another: not where we came from, but that we are all from somewhere else. Research in social identity theory suggests that even temporary group membership can have therapeutic effects, fostering trust, openness, and mutual influence. Like group therapy, these transient communities work not because individuals change each other directly, but because a sense of "us" emerges, creating psychological safety and a shared purpose of learning and becoming. In this way, travel offers a form of collective reflection and identity support, where 'common ground' and sense of belonging are momentary yet meaningful, and where growth is reinforced not in isolation, but in community.

Adapting to new environments both challenges and strengthens the brain's executive functions, particularly those involved in emotional regulation and social cognition. Cross-cultural engagement, in particular, has been shown to support the development of empathy. Interacting with diverse communities activates the brain's mirror neuron system, which helps us understand others' emotions and perspectives, deepening both relational intelligence and cultural humility. This kind of transformation is especially important in a world grappling with issues of identity on a global scale. In times marked by polarization, nationalism, and cultural misunderstanding, travel, when approached as immersion rather than consumption, offers a unique form of empathy building. It reminds us that while our lives may look different, the human experience is deeply shared. We laugh, we grieve, we struggle, we dream. And when we connect with people across boundaries - geographic, linguistic, cultural, we expand not just our awareness, but our capacity for connection. This too becomes part of who we are.

For some, travel becomes a central pillar of identity. The digital nomad, the expat, the backpacker, the cultural anthropologist, each builds a lifestyle around movement, often blending work, passion, and exploration. For others, travel serves as a temporary reset, a way to step outside the noise and return with greater clarity.

Regardless of form, the question is not whether travel shape's identity, it always does but whether we are conscious of how, and to what end. As we move forward in this book, this chapter invites readers to reflect on their own traveler identity. What role has movement played in shaping who you are? How do your experiences away from home inform your values, your relationships, your aspirations? Are you traveling to escape, or to evolve? How do you better embrace the change to our identity that travel provides? By exploring these questions, we begin to understand that identity is not something fixed. Like travel itself, it is dynamic, responsive, and deeply influenced by where and how we choose to go.

Just as travel shapes individual identity, it also shapes collective identity. Journeys shared with others, partners, families, teams, communities can become powerful accelerators of trust, bonding, and shared meaning. Joint travel experiences invite vulnerability, co-problem solving, and emotional attunement. They also create new narratives that help us explain the world. Whether on a leadership retreat, a multi-generational trip, or a spontaneous journey with friends, shared movement strengthens relational intelligence and creates collective memory. In a fragmented world, traveling together becomes a practice in co-presence and belonging.

# Identity Reinvention

Travel offers something subtle yet profound: the chance to meet ourselves outside the architecture of our everyday lives. When we step into unfamiliar environments, we are also stepping out of the roles and expectations that shape us at home - parent, leader, colleague, friend, achiever, caretaker, performer. Distance from routine becomes distance from identity. In this space, reinvention is not only possible, it is almost inevitable.

Psychologists call this the "clean slate effect": when context shifts dramatically, behavioral and cognitive patterns loosen. The neural pathways governing habit and self-concept become more plastic. This is why some people feel more confident abroad, more curious, more open, even more authentic. Travel interrupts the feedback loops that reinforce who we believe ourselves to be. Freed from the familiar mirrors that reflect our identity back to us, we glimpse versions of ourselves that were dormant or constrained.

Identity abroad becomes exploratory, elastic and in the anonymity of a new city or culture, we test edges, we speak more boldly, dress differently, say yes more often, and slowdown in ways daily life rarely permits. We discover that parts of us we thought fixed might actually be contextual. The self becomes a landscape to navigate, not a destination to protect. This does not imply abandoning who we are, but rather recognizing that we are more plural, layered and capable of becoming than routine allows.

Reinvention abroad is not escapism. It is not the construction of fantasy versions of ourselves; nor is it an avoidance of responsibility or belonging. The real power lies in returning home with the fragments of ourselves discovered elsewhere and integrating them intentionally. Growth is not the performance of a new identity, but the expansion of a truer one. Travel grants us the rare opportunity to experiment with possibility, then carry its insights into the architecture of our lives. We become, paradoxically, more ourselves by stepping away from the places that once defined us.

To travel in this way is to use movement as a mirror rather than a mask. The goal is not reinvention for the sake of novelty, but transformation rooted in awareness. Each new environment becomes a laboratory for identity, revealing who we are when expectations fall away, and who we might become when curiosity leads. In this sense, travel does not change us; it introduces us to ourselves, then invites us to choose what follows.

# The Death of the Bucket List

For decades, the "bucket list" has served as a cultural shorthand for ambition and aspiration. It represents the idea that life is a finite journey, and therefore we must collect extraordinary experiences before our time runs out. For many travelers, this has translated into a checklist of must-see destinations: the Eiffel Tower lighting up at night, Machu Picchu at dawn, the Northern Lights in Iceland.

These iconic moments, while often beautiful and moving, have also been absorbed into a broader narrative of travel as achievement, a sequence of validations to be completed, documented, and shared. But as our understanding of travel evolves, the limitations of this approach are becoming increasingly clear.

This chapter challenges the checklist mindset and proposes a more conscious, values-driven way of thinking about travel. We explore how the commodification of experience, combined with the pressures of social media and a consumerist model of modern tourism, has created a distorted view of what meaningful exploration looks like. In doing so, we call into question the assumption that quantity equals value, that more countries, more sights, and more photos automatically amount to personal growth. At the core of the bucket list approach is the psychology of goal pursuit and attainment.

According to self-determination theory, meaningful goals are those aligned with our basic needs - curiosity, connection and personal meaning. However, bucket list travel often relies heavily on extrinsic drivers. The list itself becomes a form of external scaffolding, guiding behavior not through presence or intuition, but through pre-scripted ambition, social normative pressure from a peer group (or desire to be part of a group). While achieving these goals can produce temporary satisfaction, they may not produce lasting transformation if they are not connected to the traveler's deeper values or context.

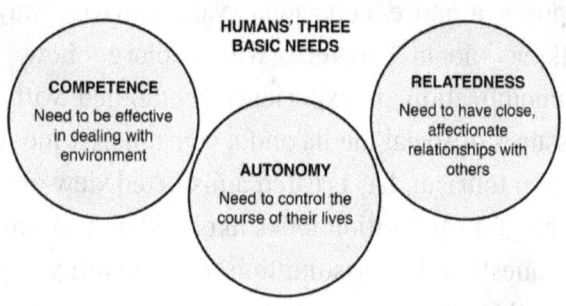

Neuroscientific studies suggest that novelty and anticipation both play significant roles in how we experience pleasure. Planning a trip, imagining what it will be like, and looking forward to it can activate reward pathways in the brain, particularly involving dopamine release. However, the repetitive pursuit of "peak" moments, one dramatic view after another can lead to what psychologists call hedonic adaptation. In some cases, this pattern can begin to mirror behavioral addiction, where the search for stimulation becomes compulsive rather than intentional.

Over time, the emotional impact of these experiences diminishes, especially if the traveler is always seeking the next rush, the excitement of the next 'to do' on the list becomes addictive, but once it's attained, its impact on self is diluted. This can lead to a cycle of pursuit without fulfillment, where the deeper emotional resonance of a place is bypassed in favor of its photographability or social currency. Retail therapy is another form of this type of behavior we see in everyday life.

Moreover, the bucket list often orients us toward outcomes rather than the processes of understanding, curiosity, learning and applying. It emphasizes having been somewhere, rather than being there. It centers attention on completion over connection. In this framework, travel becomes a form of acquisition, of stories, stamps, and experiences rather than engagement. This mindset can inadvertently flatten our experiences, making even extraordinary places feel interchangeable. A waterfall in Iceland becomes just another checkmark. A sacred temple in Bali becomes a backdrop.

We risk losing not only depth, but also the capacity to be changed. Contrast this with the psychological model of experiential processing, in which individuals immerse themselves in the present moment, attending to sensory, emotional, historical and relational aspects of experience. This mode of engagement is associated with greater well-being and deeper memory encoding. It requires slowing down, letting go of control, and being open to what unfolds. In travel, this might mean staying in one place longer, engaging in conversation with locals, or allowing for unscripted detours. It may not yield a perfect photo, but it often leads to more meaningful and lasting transformation.

The problem is not the desire to see beautiful or iconic places; this desire is human and understandable. Rather, the issue lies in the mindset of consumption, which treats these places as products rather than living, dynamic environments. The bucket list reinforces a model of travel that is extractive, rather than reciprocal.

It positions the traveler as a collector, not a participant. The same dynamic often plays out in controlled forms of travel, such as resorts or insulated tourist bubbles, where comfort and predictability can limit genuine engagement. This model does little to foster empathy, respect, or responsibility. Qualities that are increasingly essential in a globally interconnected world.

To move beyond the bucket list is not to reject ambition or the pursuit of dreams. It is to reframe ambition in terms of growth, connection, and contribution. It is to ask deeper questions: Why do I want to go there? What do I hope to learn? How will I engage with this place beyond the photograph? It also involves a shift from the monumental to the meaningful, from chasing rare spectacles to appreciating ordinary beauty. The quiet morning in a village café, the unexpected kindness of a stranger, the solitude of walking alone through unfamiliar streets. These moments, often absent from lists, are often the ones that stay with us. This reorientation aligns with broader trends in psychology and education that value process over product. It echoes the rise of mindfulness practices, slow living, and intentional design. In travel, this might mean choosing depth over breadth, staying curious rather than conclusive, and focusing less on what we've "done" and more on what we've noticed, felt, and understood.

## MINDSET FOR THE FUTURE

The future of travel demands a more reflective approach. Climate change, cultural sensitivity, and the mental health of travelers all point toward a model that is slower, more deliberate, and more aware. Moving beyond the bucket list does not mean abandoning dreams. It means choosing them more wisely and living them more fully. In doing so, we allow travel to become what it has always had the potential to be: not just a journey across landscapes, but a deeper journey inward.

This shift also parallels a broader global need: moving from extractive to regenerative travel. Conscious travel asks not only, "What will this place give me?" but also, "How will my presence impact this place socially, culturally, ecologically?" Regenerative travel is not charity or guilt-based tourism, it is reciprocity. It is learning from communities rather than consuming them, participating rather than passing through, and leaving ecosystems and cultures healthier for having been engaged with. Small choices, slower travel, local economies, respectful attention become acts of stewardship. Travelers evolve from takers to partners in sustaining the world they explore.

# The Value of Intentional Travel

If the bucket list represents accumulation, intentional travel represents awareness. It moves us beyond the idea of travel as accomplishment and toward travel as alignment between our inner landscape and the world we choose to enter. It asks us not simply Where do I want to go? But who do I want to become through this journey?

## MINDSET FOR THE FUTURE

At its heart, intentional travel is a philosophy of attention. It understands that the quality of any experience is shaped not by scale or spectacle, but by presence. A sunrise witnessed with attention can be more meaningful than a world wonder seen in haste. A single conversation held with openness can shift us more than a dozen photographs ever will. Intent transforms movement into meaning.

To travel with intention is to treat each journey as a dialogue. With place. With history. With community. With self. Instead of consuming destinations, we enter them with curiosity, humility, and reciprocity. We listen before we assume. We observe before we conclude. we ask, what does this place need from me, not only what can I take from it?

This shift is not subtle; it changes everything. It alters how we plan, how we move, how we remember.

When planning, intentionality reframes choice. Rather than defaulting to trending locations or borrowed desires, we pause.

We ask:

- What is calling me and why?
- What personal question or longing sits underneath this destination?

- Is this journey about escape, expansion, healing, belonging, curiosity, or rest?

Psychological research shows that when experiences are tied to personal meaning, we engage more deeply, learn more fully, and internalize memories more richly. Intention primes perception. It acts like a compass, orienting our attention toward what matters most. Suddenly, travel becomes less about escape and more about encounters both outward and inward.

During travel, conscious attention changes how we behave. We slow down; we observe nuance. We allow for uncertainty rather than controlling every detail. We hold space for the texture of a place, its rhythm, its tone, its hidden layers. Instead of rushing to check off a list, we make space for what cannot be anticipated: serendipity, invitation, surprise, challenge. We trust that part of the journey will reveal itself only when we are quite enough to receive it.

This kind of travel also invites personal accountability. We consider our footprint not only ecological, but emotional and cultural. We support local economies, honor customs, and choose experiences that uplift rather than extract. We show up not as spectators, but as respectful guests.

Most importantly, intentional travel deepens return. Without intention, travel becomes a memory archive - stories, photos, fragments. With intention, travel becomes integration, lessons, shifts, a new way of being. We come home not simply enriched, but rearranged. Something inside has widened. Something unnecessary has fallen away. A thread of insight has begun to shape how we live, lead, relate, and decide.

Travel becomes a practice, not an event, and when travel becomes a practice, it changes our everyday life. We begin to approach home with the same curiosity we once reserved for elsewhere. The familiar becomes layered again. We notice. We ask. We appreciate. We move through daily routines with more intention, more patience, more reverence. Travel stops being something we step into and out of, and instead becomes a mindset we carry.

In this way, intentional travel is not opposed to adventure, it refines it. It does not diminish ambition, it roots it. It does not reject exploration; it expands its meaning. It reminds us that wonder is not a commodity, awe is not a checklist, and belonging cannot be purchased. Intentional travel asks us to be fully present to bring all of ourselves to the world, and to allow the world to shape us in return. It honors that travel is not merely a movement through space, but a movement through self.

In an age where movement can be instant, mindless, and extractive, intentional travel is an act of resistance. It rejects the hurried, curated, performative approach to place, and instead chooses depth over density, presence over performance, and transformation over accumulation.

It invites us to remember that meaningful travel is not measured by distance, prestige or the number of places we can see in a short vacation, but by attention, reciprocity, and inner shift. The most valuable journeys are not those that take us the farthest, but those that bring us closest to place, to people, and to who we are becoming.

# Regenerative Travel

If intentional travel asks us why we move, regenerative travel asks us how we leave. It invites us beyond the idea of treading lightly and into the practice of leaving places better than we found them socially, culturally, environmentally, and relationally. It shifts travel from a personal pursuit to a shared stewardship, acknowledging that every journey creates ripples in the ecosystems and communities we enter.

Regenerative travel starts with humility. It means remembering we're stepping into stories that existed long before us. Each place has memory, lineage, rhythm, and fragility. To move through it is a privilege that comes with responsibility not only to protect, but to enrich, to uplift, to contribute. We arrive not as consumers, but as temporary caretakers.

This mindset reframes our presence. Instead of asking "What can this place give me?", regenerative travelers ask, "How can my presence contribute to the flourishing of this place, its people, its land, its culture, its future?" Contribution does not always take grand form; often, it lives in micro-acts of respect, curiosity, accountability, and reciprocity. The way we listen. The businesses we support. The patience we practice. The conversations we hold. The stories we share when we return and how we choose to tell them.

To travel regeneratively is to recognize interdependence. Healthy destinations are living systems: nature, culture, economy, identity, tradition, innovation, and community intertwined. When one frays, the rest strain. True regenerative travel supports this symbiosis, it honors Indigenous knowledge, values local governance, uplifts local labor and ownership, and understands that cultural preservation is as vital as ecological protection. It turns tourism into a facilitator and collaborator rather than a disruptor.

This approach stands in direct contrast to extractive tourism, the kind that treats destinations as consumable and replaceable, that rewards volume over depth, spectacle over substance. Regenerative travel calls us to move differently: slower, deeper, more relationally. To choose fewer places, but know them more wholly. To ask before photographing. To sit in local cafes. To listen to histories that never make it into guidebooks. To learn names. To understand what communities, celebrate and what they grieve.

Regenerative travel doesn't end at departure. How we return matters. What insights do we bring home? What habits do we shift? How do we honor the lessons of a place when we are no longer in it? Regeneration continues in the way we live at home in how we support local ecology, engage with diverse communities, and cultivate belonging and respect where we live. Regeneration is not only an act of travel; it is a way of inhabiting the world. It invites us to consider our footprint not only in miles but in meaning. To understand that our lives like journeys leave traces, and that we have agency in shaping the quality of those traces.

## THE MEANING OF TRAVEL IS CHANGING

In a time when global mobility holds both extraordinary potential and extraordinary consequence, regenerative travel offers a compass. It points us toward practices that heal rather than harm, connect rather than divide, restore rather than deplete. It reminds us that travel is not escape; it is engagement. Not indulgence but interconnection. And that the true measure of a journey is not what we bring home, but what we leave behind: understanding, respect, dignity, and a trace of care. Some of the most meaningful footprints are, and will be, the ones we help others stand upon.

# Travel as Privilege - Accessibility, Inequality, and Responsibility

Travel opens consciousness, but it is not an equal opportunity.
It is shaped by access - economic, political, physical, and social. While we celebrate travel as expansion, curiosity, and growth, we must also recognize that the freedom to move is not universal.

- Passports are not all equal.
- Borders do not welcome everyone.
- Mobility is a resource unevenly distributed, historically inherited, and deeply tied to power.

For many, travel is a choice. Whether that's a holiday, moving home, or a journey of self-exploration. For others, movement is forced migration, displacement, crisis, survival. And for many more, travel remains a dream out of reach.

This reality does not diminish the value of travel but it demands a conscious traveler. One who recognizes privilege not as guilt, but as responsibility. To move with humility. To notice who is visible in travel narratives and who is missing. To understand that the ability to explore freely is a gift, not an entitlement.

Travel privilege doesn't arise from personal circumstances alone. It is shaped by multiple layers of influence, from family and community to national policy and global power structures. Ecological Systems Theory helps map these layers, showing how mobility is shaped by forces far beyond individual choice.

# ECOLOGICAL SYSTEMS THEORY

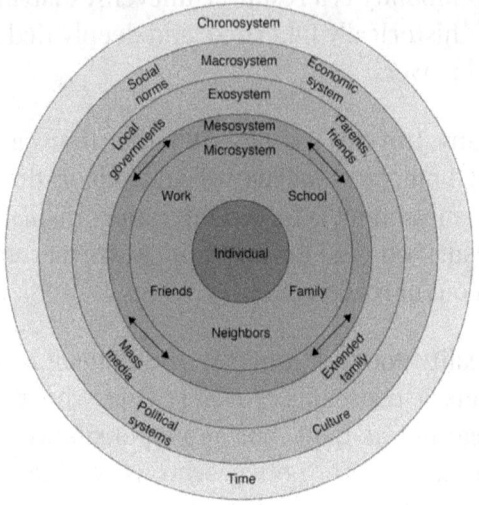

Accessibility also stretches beyond economics and passports. Physical ability, neurodiversity, gender identity, social background, each shapes the experience of moving through the world. Safety is not evenly felt. Comfort is not universal. Exploration does not land the same for everybody.

To travel consciously is to ask:

- Who does travel include? Who does it exclude?
- How do we make movement more equitable, not just more efficient?

We cannot democratize every border or undo centuries of inequality with awareness alone. But we can travel with integrity, choosing systems that uplift rather than extract, supporting local mobility initiatives, advocating for inclusive access, and acknowledging the layers of privilege in our journeys. When we recognize travel as privilege, we transform it from consumption into appreciation, from entitlement into stewardship, and from individual pursuit into shared possibility. Travel, then, becomes not just where we go but how we move toward a world where freedom of movement is not a luxury, but a right of passage.

## Considerations for the Conscious Traveler

To integrate the ideas in Part 1, consider:

- What is the real purpose behind my travel choices?
- Do I choose destinations based on curiosity or validation?
- Where am I prioritizing comfort over growth, and how might I rebalance?
- How can I leave places, cultures, and communities better than I found them?

- Who do I become when I travel alongside others and how do I support shared growth?
- How do I measure the success of a journey beyond photos or tick boxes?
- What is one way I can deepen presence, slow down, or engage more meaningfully on my next trip?

Travel is no longer simply mobility. It is a mindset, a moral orientation, and a developmental practice. How we move through the world increasingly reflects how we move through life.

In the next section, we'll shift our focus to the cognitive and emotional transformations that occur when we enter unfamiliar environments. We'll explore how novelty, challenge, and discomfort rewire the brain and how being out of place might be exactly what we need to grow into who we are

# PART 2

# The Mind on The Move

"It's the little details that are vital. Little things make big things happen."

*John Wooden*

What happens to the mind when we step outside the familiar? When the scenery changes, routines dissolve, and expectations no longer hold?

As we move through this section, it becomes clear that travel is not merely leisure or escape, it becomes a neurological apprenticeship in adaptability, emotional intelligence, and perspective shifting. In a world where workplaces demand agility, societies require cross-cultural awareness, and leaders must navigate uncertainty with steadiness. The cognitive benefits of meaningful travel are not peripheral, they are strategic. The future will reward those who can regulate emotions, question assumptions, and stay curious under pressure and travel remains one of humanity's most powerful, accessible training grounds for those capacities.

Part 2 explores how the psychological and neurological systems that shape our thoughts, emotions, and behaviors are directly influenced by movement, especially movement into unfamiliar environments. While the previous section examined why we travel and how that journey connects to identity, this section turns inward, focusing on the mental and emotional transformations that unfold through the lived experience of being away from home. Travel challenges our sense of stability. It takes us out of our comfort zone, introducing uncertainty, disrupting predictability, and demanding attention in ways daily life often does not. These very conditions, what we often label as "discomfort" are also the ones that activate growth.

Drawing from neuroscience, we examine how the brain responds to novelty, ambiguity, and awe. From the firing of mirror neurons in cross-cultural interactions to the role of the hippocampus in spatial and emotional memory, we begin to understand travel as a cognitive accelerator: it stretches our attention, rewires our perceptions, and opens neural pathways for empathy, flexibility, and insight. This section also explores the emotional dimensions of being in unfamiliar spaces. Uncertainty can be deeply uncomfortable, yet it is often where we learn the most about the world and about ourselves.

Through concepts like productive discomfort, attention restoration, and the neuroscience of awe, we unpack why these states, though mentally taxing, are vital for long-term growth. The intensity of a foreign environment sharpens our senses and can restore cognitive engagement lost in routine. Even fleeting, seemingly "little" moments, getting lost in a city, navigating a cultural faux pas, witnessing something profoundly beautiful, leave an imprint not just on memory, but on how we think and who we become. Importantly, this section looks beyond the individual. The mind on the move is also a social mind, one that must adapt to new social norms, languages, and shared spaces. In doing so, it strengthens its capacity for perspective-taking, emotional regulation, and complex communication. These are not just travel skills; they are human skills, increasingly necessary in a world that demands cross-cultural fluency, resilience, and continuous learning.

In Part 2, we invite readers to embrace travel not only as a form of exploration but as a mental discipline, a practice that demands awareness, openness, and the willingness to stretch beyond what is comfortable. When seen through the lens of neuroscience and psychology, travel becomes more than movement through space. It becomes an active rewiring of perception, belief, and identity. And in that process, the traveler is not just changed by where they go, they are changed by how deeply they are willing to engage with uncertainty itself.

# Discomfort as Growth

We rarely grow in comfort. True transformation often begins in moments of tension - those disorienting experiences when we are pulled out of familiar rhythms and forced to confront the unknown. Travel, at its best, is a deliberate stepping into such territory. Whether it's navigating a language barrier, adjusting to a new culture, or simply being far from home, the discomforts of travel are not just incidental; they are in their essence by design. They initiate cognitive, emotional, and behavioral shifts that allow us to rethink assumptions, build resilience, and expand our mental models.

Discomfort in travel comes in many forms. It may be physical, including jet lag, unfamiliar food, or the absence of basic conveniences. It may be emotional, such as loneliness, vulnerability, or the loss of routine. It may also be cognitive moments when cultural norms clash with our expectations, when systems function differently than we're used to, or when we find ourselves uncertain of how to behave. These experiences can unsettle us, and at times even provoke anxiety or doubt, but they are also rich with possibility. The issue is how we cope with them not only as a traveler in a new environment but how we respond to them as a local observing and living with tourism around us

When we face discomfort on the road, our minds automatically try to interpret what the experience means. This is where the cognitive appraisal model becomes useful. It explains how we assess a situation, whether we see it as a threat or as a challenge and how that interpretation shapes our emotional response. In the context of travel, this model helps us understand why the same moment can feel overwhelming to one person and expansive to another.

## COGNITIVE APPRAISAL MODEL
*"STRESS AS THREAT" VS "STRESS AS GROWTH CHALLENGE"*

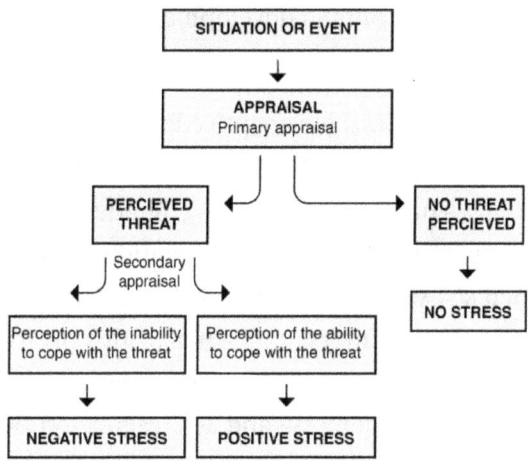

There is an emerging paradox in modern travel culture: in our pursuit of comfort, efficiency, and perceived safety, we may be unintentionally restricting the very conditions that enable growth. When travel becomes hyper-controlled, curated itineraries, insulated resorts, predictable schedules, we reduce exposure to healthy uncertainty and, over time, risk a kind of social and psychological atrophy. The instinct to avoid discomfort can erode resilience, limit cross-cultural empathy, and diminish curiosity. The future of travel mindset requires reclaiming a tolerance for the unknown not recklessly, but intentionally, recognizing that adaptability, humility, and courage are muscles strengthened only through use. In a world increasingly optimized for ease, choosing a challenge becomes a radical practice in human development.

From a psychological perspective, discomfort creates the conditions for adaptive learning, a process that forces the mind to reorganize and respond creatively. This process is grounded in the neuroscience of stress and adaptation. Moderate, controlled stress, known as eustress can stimulate the brain's learning centers, particularly the prefrontal cortex and hippocampus. These regions are involved in decision-making, memory, and self-regulation. When we face unfamiliar challenges in travel, these areas are activated, prompting us to re-evaluate our strategies, regulate emotions, and problem-solve in real time. Importantly, repeated exposure to manageable stress can increase what psychologists call cognitive flexibility, the brain's ability to shift perspectives and adapt to changing rules or contexts.

Cognitive flexibility is not just a travel asset; it is a core component of resilience, creativity, and psychological well-being. Discomfort also reveals the limits of our internal schemas; those mental shortcuts and assumptions we use to interpret the world. Schema theory in psychology suggests that we build mental frameworks based on prior experiences. These frameworks help us navigate daily life efficiently, but they can also restrict us, filtering new information through old patterns. Travel disrupts these schemas. It exposes us to alternative ways of living, thinking, and organizing society. This can be uncomfortable, challenging our beliefs about time, communication, food, family, or freedom but it is also where growth occurs. When our existing frameworks no longer explain what we're seeing or feeling, we are forced to adapt to revise or expand the way we understand the world.

At a behavioral level, discomfort encourages the development of problem-solving skills. Consider the traveler who must navigate a public transportation system in a foreign city, or find accommodation after a missed connection. These tasks, while often frustrating, build executive function, the ability to plan, organize, and manage time and resources effectively. They also foster a sense of agency: the internal belief that one is capable of handling life's complexities. This sense of agency, or self-efficacy, is a strong predictor of mental resilience and long-term motivation. Emotionally, discomfort cultivates humility. It reminds us that we are not always in control, that we do not always know best, and that our ways are not the only ways. This recognition often brought about through embarrassment, awe, or confusion is the entry point to greater empathy.

In cross-cultural settings, humility opens us to learn from others rather than impose our beliefs and way of doing things onto them. It softens judgment and makes space for mutual understanding. Socially, this shift supports the development of intercultural competence, the ability to communicate and collaborate effectively across differences. Importantly, not all discomfort is beneficial. Distress that overwhelms the nervous system due to fear, danger, or sustained isolation can impede learning and reinforce defensiveness.

For travel to become a growth experience there is a simple formula, discomfort must exist and it must be accompanied by psychological safety. This can come from preparation, support networks, reflective practice, or simply the belief that the challenge is meaningful and temporary. When these conditions are met, discomfort shifts from something to avoid to something to engage with deliberately. When these conditions are not met, situations arise when travelers resort to gregarious actions aimed at preserving what they believe is right (based on their cultural norms) over those norms of the place that they are visiting.

The resulting behavior is what we see play out in the media, including defiance of rules in visiting cities, defacing ancient ruins, destroying delicate natural environments, and anti-social behavior towards locals.

Our views of what or who are 'good' or 'bad' has also impacted our travel mindset, polarities in world views and negative perceptions regarding foreigners of any description amplifies the reactions of both travelers and locals alike. Similarly, the increasing way in which we travel today, being part of packaged tours, staying in gated resort complexes or even taking a cruise with only pockets of free time to 'explore' is further exacerbating this growth impediment quite simply because no discomfort exists in this form of travel to stretch our intercultural tolerance.

This engagement is often described as the "stretch zone", a space between comfort and panic where learning and transformation are most likely to occur. In educational psychology, this concept is closely tied to transformative learning theory, which suggests that adults grow most profoundly when their core beliefs are challenged and reexamined. Travel, when approached with intention, places us squarely in this zone. It invites us not only to stretch, but to reflect, to ask what we are learning, how we are changing, and what those changes mean for how we live.

Discomfort is not a flaw in the travel experience, nor does it mean that we've done something wrong, it is a feature that should be embraced. It is the catalyst that forces us to reorient, reframe, and rebuild. In a world increasingly shaped by complexity, ambiguity, and global interconnection, the capacity to navigate discomfort is a critical skill. Travel offers us a unique training ground, a space where we can practice this skill in real time, supported by curiosity, novelty, and stillness, in the awareness that every challenge is also an invitation.

# Attention in New Environments

One of the most immediate cognitive effects of travel is a shift in how we pay attention. In our daily environments, much of what we perceive becomes automated. The brain, designed for efficiency, quickly filters out familiar stimuli to conserve energy for novelty or threat. This is known as habituation, a neurological process that dulls our sensitivity to repeated input. While this serves a functional purpose, it also means that much of everyday life is lived on autopilot. Travel disrupts this pattern. New environments force the brain out of habitual attention modes and into heightened states of awareness.

When we enter unfamiliar surroundings, and experience different languages, architectural styles, sounds, smells, and social cues, our attentional system responds by becoming more active and alert.

The reticular activating system (RAS) in the brainstem plays a crucial role in this process, acting as a gatekeeper that prioritizes novel or emotionally significant stimuli. As a result, travelers often report feeling more present, more observant, and more attuned to detail. The ordinary becomes extraordinary because it is no longer filtered through routine. This increased attentional engagement has both cognitive and emotional benefits. From a cognitive perspective, it improves sensory integration and supports stronger memory encoding. New experiences that are vividly attended to are more likely to be stored in long-term memory, particularly when they involve multisensory inputs. This is why we often remember seemingly small moments while traveling, such as a conversation in a market, the color of the sky, the sound of unfamiliar music. These memories are not only richer; they also contribute to a deeper sense of place and meaning.

Emotionally, focused attention enhances mindfulness, the capacity to be fully present and aware without judgment. While mindfulness is often cultivated through formal practice, it can also emerge spontaneously during travel, especially when we are immersed in a setting that demands our full cognitive participation. The unfamiliar asks us to slow down, to observe, and to listen. This presence not only deepens the quality of the experience, it also creates space for reflection, insight, and emotional regulation.

Research in psychology has shown that attention restoration, the process of recovering from mental fatigue, can be supported by exposure to novel or aesthetically engaging environments. Originally associated with natural settings, this theory has been expanded to include any context that provides a sense of "soft fascination," or gentle engagement of attention without cognitive overload.

## ATTENTION RESTORATION THEORY
*(ART)*

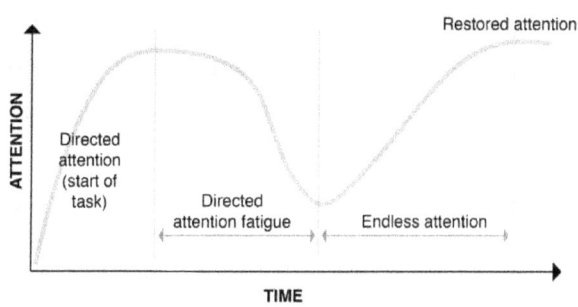

For travelers, this can occur in urban landscapes, cultural spaces, or even during transit. The key is that attention is shifted from goal-directed focus to open, exploratory awareness, a mode of thinking associated with creativity, insight, and stress recovery. However, the attentional benefits of travel are not automatic. They can be undermined by distraction, over-scheduling, or digital saturation.

In recent years, the proliferation of mobile technology and social media has introduced a paradox: while we have more tools than ever to navigate and document our experiences, we also face unprecedented pressure to multitask and perform – the 'need to do everything now' syndrome. This cognitive load can fragment attention and reduce our capacity to engage with the moment. The challenge, then, is to protect and cultivate attentional presence amid the noise. One way to do this is by embracing attentional intention, the practice of choosing where and how we focus. This might involve slowing down, limiting digital engagement, or setting micro-intentions for each day of a journey. It can also include reflective practices such as journaling, sketching, or contemplative walking. These activities support attention, strengthen memory consolidation, and increase the emotional weight of the experiences we have.

Attention is also amplified by who we travel with. Shared experience activates social bonding mechanisms, deepens emotional encoding, and strengthens relational memory. Travel partners, families, and leadership groups often report accelerated trust, vulnerability, and connection, because navigating new environments requires communication, patience, and co-regulation. These relational experiences are not incidental; they are neurological and emotional training grounds. In this way, travel fosters collective intelligence as much as individual insight, reminding us that movement can be a shared evolution, not only a solo journey.

From a neuroscience standpoint, sustained attention in novel environments strengthens neural networks related to executive function and emotional regulation. The prefrontal cortex, responsible for planning and self-control, is particularly engaged when we manage competing stimuli in new settings. Over time, this strengthens attentional endurance and cognitive resilience. In a world increasingly characterized by distraction, the ability to focus, to notice, to remain present is a powerful skill. Ultimately, travel reintroduces us to our own capacity for attention. It reveals how much we miss when we are consumed by habit and competing stimuli in our everyday lives, and how much richness is available when we look with new eyes. It trains the mind to be more agile, more receptive, and more alive to the world around us.

In the next chapter, we explore one of the most profound psychological states that travel can induce: awe. We'll examine the neuroscience behind awe-inspiring moments, how they alter our sense of self, and why they hold such powerful potential for mindset transformation.

# The Neuroscience of Awe

Some travel moments defy language. Standing at the edge of the Grand Canyon, walking around the Acropolis, witnessing the Aurora Borealis dance across the sky, these experiences don't just impress us; they change us. They shake our assumptions, suspend our inner dialogue, and momentarily expand our perception of what's possible. This feeling, known as awe, is not just a poetic flourish. It is a measurable, neurologically grounded experience that plays a critical role in mindset development and personal growth.

Awe is often described as a response to vastness, something physically, conceptually, or spiritually immense that challenges our existing mental models. Psychologists Dacher Keltner and Jonathan Haidt define awe as an emotional response to perceptual vastness that requires accommodation. In other words, awe occurs when we encounter something so extraordinary that our current understanding cannot easily absorb it. The brain responds by working to reorganize its frameworks, creating new cognitive and emotional space.

Flow Theory helps explain why some travel moments feel deeply absorbing while others leave us disengaged or overwhelmed. It maps how the balance between challenge and skill shapes our emotional state, from boredom to anxiety to full immersion. For example, navigating a busy market in Marrakech may feel overwhelming at first, but as your confidence grows and you understand the rhythms of the place, that same environment can shift from anxiety to flow, becoming one of the most memorable parts of the journey.

# FLOW THEORY

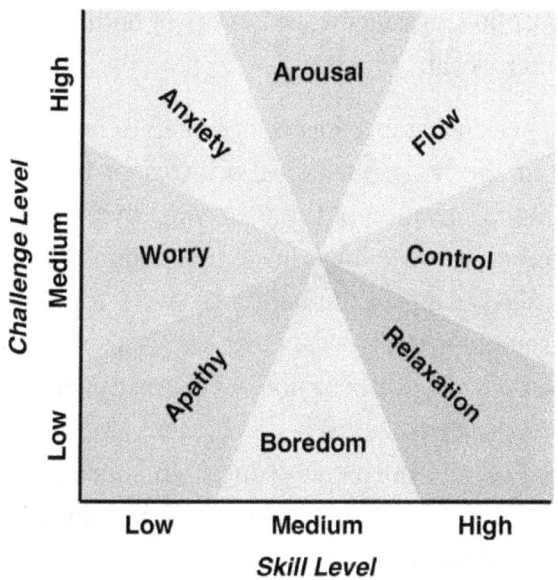

From a neuroscientific perspective, awe engages several key systems in the brain. Functional MRI studies show that during awe experiences, activity decreases in the default mode network (DMN), the same network involved in self-referential thought (i.e. how we relate external information to ourselves). When this system quiets, we experience a reduction in the ego and a sense of connection to something larger. This helps explain why awe is often accompanied by feelings of humility, wonder, and unity. At the same time, awe activates the prefrontal cortex and insula, which are involved in emotional regulation and interoception, enhancing awareness of both the outer and inner world.

Experiencing awe has been linked to measurable shifts in the body, including changes in heart rate variability, activation of the parasympathetic nervous system, and reductions in inflammation markers. These shifts support the body's recovery from stress and promote overall well-being. Awe is also linked to increased prosocial behavior - generosity, empathy, and cooperation as well as higher levels of life satisfaction and open-mindedness. In short, awe not only feels good; it also makes us more cognitively flexible and socially attuned.

Travel is uniquely positioned to generate awe because it places us in environments where the extraordinary becomes accessible. This might be through natural phenomena, monumental architecture, cultural rituals, or deeply human encounters that defy expectation. Importantly, awe is not reserved for grand spectacles. It can be found in a quiet moment of beauty, a gesture of kindness, or the realization of shared humanity across cultural boundaries. What matters is not the scale, but the perception of vastness and the emotional openness of the observer.

The psychological benefits of awe extend to how we process information and make decisions. In awe states, individuals tend to perceive time more expansively, experience a sense of mental clarity, and become more willing to revise their beliefs. This has important implications for learning and mindset. By destabilizing rigid frameworks, awe invites curiosity and humility. It creates a space where the unfamiliar is not feared, but welcomed, a crucial attitude in a complex, fast-changing world. Moreover, awe has a profound effect on identity. As the ego recedes, we are more likely to experience self-transcendence, a shift from self-centered awareness to a more relational or collective orientation. This does not mean loss of self, but rather an expansion of perspective that allows for greater empathy and connection, a feeling of belonging and social identity in a community.

In travel, these moments can create lasting changes in how we relate to others and to the planet. Many travelers return from awe-inducing experiences with renewed appreciation for nature, different cultures, or the fragility of life itself. Of course, awe cannot be manufactured on demand. It is inherently elusive, and attempts to engineer it through overplanning or constant stimulation can often backfire. Instead, awe tends to emerge when we are open, present, and willing to be surprised. Travel encourages this by placing us in states of heightened attention and uncertainty conditions that are ripe for awe if we are paying attention.

This is where intentional travel design comes into play: not in scripting every detail, but in creating space for the unscripted to emerge. To travel with awe is to travel with humility, curiosity, and reverence. It is to acknowledge that the world is more complex, beautiful, and mysterious than we can fully grasp. It is to embrace the smallness of the self not as a limitation, but as a doorway to deeper connection. Awe also creates an opening for regenerative thinking. When we are humbled by beauty, scale, culture, or nature, we become more attuned to our responsibility within it. This shift moves us from being passive recipients of inspiration to active caretakers of place. Awe awakens reciprocity. It encourages travelers to ask: how can my presence contribute rather than consume? How do I leave a community, ecosystem, or cultural space better than I found it? Awe, then, is not only an emotional reward, it is a gateway to stewardship, civic consciousness, and regenerative travel values. And it is to recognize that in those fleeting, expansive moments when we are truly awestruck, we are also most alive.

The concept and science of awe is an important consideration for the packaged tour industry sector. How a travel itinerary is curated needs to consider what can be left for 'surprise' without being too scripted and too certain. In essence awe is good for business. The traveler who experiences awe on a tour is more likely to talk about their experience to others, be able to recall every detail, and associate such a rewarding experience with the tour company that helped facilitate that.

In the next chapter, we examine how memory, place, and meaning intersect. We'll explore how the brain encodes travel experiences, why certain locations become unforgettable, and how meaning is constructed through the emotional resonance of place.

# Memory, Place and Meaning

Where we go is often less important than what we carry home. Long after a journey ends, certain places stay with us not just as images, but as emotional landmarks encoded into our personal history. We remember not only what we saw, but how we felt: the color of the light, the tone of a voice, the feeling of standing in a foreign square at dusk. These memories are not passive; they form part of our identity and sense of meaning. In this chapter, we explore how the brain encodes experiences of place, why some locations leave a lasting psychological imprint, and how meaning is constructed through memory in the context of travel.

Human memory is fundamentally spatial. The hippocampus, a seahorse-shaped structure deep in the brain, plays a central role in memory formation and spatial navigation. Neuroscientific studies have shown that the hippocampus functions like a cognitive map, linking emotions, events, and physical environments into cohesive memory networks. This is why location and memory are so tightly bound: we remember events more vividly when we can visualize where they happened. Travel, by introducing us to novel, richly textured environments, provides an ideal context for deep memory encoding. Place-based memories are also strengthened by emotional salience.

When we experience something emotionally significant, joy, awe, surprise, or even fear, the amygdala, another key brain structure, works alongside the hippocampus to encode that event more robustly. This is why travel memories are often charged with feeling. A sunrise hike in a remote mountain range, a spontaneous conversation on a bus with a stranger, or the quiet solitude of a sacred space, these moments often become more than memories. They become markers of meaning.

The theory of episodic memory, our ability to recall specific events with contextual detail, further explains why travel stands out in our mental timeline.

Unlike routine events, travel disrupts the monotony of daily life and introduces unique cues that make episodes more distinct. These cues, new smells, languages, and visual landscapes act as anchors, making it easier for the brain to recall the associated emotional and narrative details. In fact, research suggests that people often perceive time as moving more slowly during travel, not because of any physical change, but because of the density of encoded experiences.

From a psychological standpoint, travel provides what Viktor Frankl referred to as meaningful moments, brief but powerful experiences that help individuals make sense of their lives. These moments are often tied to a sense of "place." Whether it's a landscape that mirrors our internal state, a city that resonates with a hidden part of ourselves, or a cultural ritual that connects us to something ancient, these experiences evoke a form of existential clarity. They affirm our place in the world and often prompt reflection about purpose, connection, or direction.

Travel also enables what psychologists call autobiographical reasoning the ability to construct a coherent life narrative by linking past experiences with future intentions. Meaningful places become chapters in this narrative. We do not simply recall them; we return to them in memory to draw insight, to remember who we were at the time, and to understand how we've changed. These place-based memories can become a source of strength and continuity, especially in times of transition or uncertainty.

The construction of meaning is not purely internal; it is also social. We often share our travel experiences through storytelling, photographs, or rituals of remembrance. In doing so, we reinforce and refine their significance. These acts of narration help consolidate memory and embed it more deeply into identity. They also allow others to enter into our experiences, to co-create meaning through listening, reflection, or shared memory. This is why returning to a place with someone we love, or telling a story about a solo journey, can be just as powerful as the trip itself. It can even be therapeutic.

Culturally, certain places carry collective memory histories, symbols, or sacredness that transcend individual experience. Visiting these places can evoke profound emotional responses, even if we are not personally connected to their history. Standing at a historic monument, entering a revered temple, or walking through a memorial site can create a sense of temporal depth and connection to something larger than ourselves. These experiences often resonate deeply because they bridge personal and collective meaning.

Of course, not all travel experiences leave deep memories. Some fade quickly, particularly when they are rushed, distracted, or lacking emotional engagement. The quality of attention we bring to a place directly influences how we will remember it. This reinforces the value of mindful travel of being present, slowing down, and allowing ourselves to fully feel and absorb our surroundings. When we do, even the simplest moments, a meal, a quiet walk, a conversation can become lasting imprints.

In essence, travel teaches us that memory is not just about recording events; it is about encoding meaning. The places we go shape how we remember, and how we remember shapes who we become. The most powerful journeys are not those that fill a passport, but those that fill the mind with questions, insights, and connections that remain long after the return flight.

Memory, place and meaning has significant considerations for the traveler when preparing an itinerary for an upcoming trip: It may feel 'necessary' to pack in as many places, and sights in a 10-day visit to feel that the travel cost and time away was 'worth it'.

However, what we now know about meaning, it's not about the quantity of things to do when away, it's about the space we give ourselves to connect the place and its meaning to our own. So, reshaping our itineraries where we move less and take in more creates far more value than sight-hopping ever can.

# Stillness & Retreat

In a world that equates movement with meaning, stillness can feel almost radical. Travel is often imagined as motion - planes, trains, calendars full, schedules dense with experience. Yet some of the most transformative journeys unfold not in motion, but in deliberate pause. Retreats, sabbaticals, periods of solitude in unfamiliar places, they offer a different kind of travel, one defined not by accumulation but by subtraction. What happens when we let the world come to us instead of rushing toward it?

## THE MIND ON THE MOVE

Stillness in travel is not idleness. It is a quiet attunement, a retreat from the noise of our identities, responsibilities, and routines. Neuroscience shows that when external stimuli decrease, internal processing accelerates. The default mode network activates, enabling deeper introspection, meaning-making, and emotional integration. In stillness, the dust of constant motion settles and what we truly feel, fear, or long for begins to surface. Retreat becomes a laboratory for inner clarity.

Many cultures have long understood the power of traveling to pause. Monastic traditions, pilgrimages with intentional rest, Indigenous practices of withdrawal to land, all treat stillness as a form of journeying. Modern life, however, often denies us this space. We move quickly, consume rapidly, and mistake pace for purpose. Stillness reminds us that spaciousness itself can be a destination. A silent morning in a remote village, a quiet apartment in a foreign city, a walk without phone or agenda, these are not gaps in experience; they are gateways.

Retreat also reshapes our relationship with time. Away from productivity culture, time expands. Minutes stretch, attention deepens, the nervous system recalibrates. This deceleration can feel uncomfortable at first; boredom and restlessness surface before insight and presence emerge. Yet such discomfort is often the doorway to renewal. In stillness we listen: to the world, to our body, to our intuition. We reconnect with desires and questions muted by busyness.

To travel in stillness is to honor the inner landscape as much as the outer one. It is a reclaiming of agency, the choice to be present rather than propelled, to absorb rather than accumulate. Stillness invites us to see ourselves not as tourists moving through the world, but as witnesses being moved by it. When we return from such quiet journeys, we bring with us a steadiness that enhances how we navigate movement, noise, and change. In this way, stillness is not the opposite of travel, but its deepening. We learn that exploration does not always require motion; sometimes the most profound transformation occurs in silence, in stillness, in surrender to presence itself.

# Micro-Exploration - Depth over Distance

Not all journeys unfold across continents. Some happen on a single street, during a short walk, or in the quiet act of noticing what we usually ignore. Micro-exploration is the practice of treating the familiar as foreign by replacing scale with depth, distance with presence. In a culture that equates travel with grand itineraries and far-flung escapes, micro-exploration reminds us that discovery begins with attention, not geography.

Psychologically, novelty and meaning are not tied to distance. Neuroscience shows that what stimulates the brain is not the size of the journey, but the degree of engagement. When we shift how we see, pausing to observe light on a building, listening to a stranger's cadence, following a path we've never taken in our own city, we activate the same neural pathways that fire in distant travel. The unfamiliar exists everywhere; we simply stop noticing it close to home.

Micro-exploration cultivates the traveler's mindset in daily life. It asks us to step outside our habitual routes and perceptual shortcuts. The goal is not efficiency but curiosity. Try walking without headphones. Take a different commute. Enter a shop you've passed a hundred times but never entered. Sit on a bench and watch for patterns: how people greet each other, how languages mix, how time moves in a place where you are still instead of rushing. These small acts of attention sharpen the mind and soften the ego. They remind us that wonder is not a resource tied to an airfare.

There is humility in small journeys. They teach us that our world, no matter how ordinary it seems, is layered, dynamic, and alive. A tree we never noticed before becomes a marker of season and time. A neighbor's ritual becomes a story of belonging. A quiet café becomes a portal to new characters and conversations. Micro-exploration dissolves the binary between "home" and "away," inviting us to see the world not as a series of destinations, but as an ongoing field of discovery.

This practice also has a grounding effect. In an age of rapid movement and digital distraction, micro-exploration builds presence muscles. It keeps travel from becoming escapism and turns it into a way of being an attention posture rather than a logistical event. It prepares us for deeper travel by teaching patience, observation, and empathy in familiar spaces, where preconceptions can be hardest to challenge. When we finally travel far, we arrive more open, more attuned, more capable of seeing nuance.

Ultimately, micro-exploration democratizes exploration. It removes the barriers of cost, time, and status. It reminds us that a traveler is not someone who goes far, but someone who looks closely. The world expands not only when we cross borders, but when we cross the thresholds of our own habits. Through small journeys, we learn that movement is not required for awakening, attention is. And in training ourselves to find the extraordinary in the everyday, we prepare for a future where the meaning of travel is measured not in miles, but in perception, humility, and depth.

This depth-driven model of travel also reflects a different kind of return on investment, one measured in clarity, perspective, relationships, and emotional expansion rather than consumption or mileage. As travel becomes more intentional, immersive, and reflective, its value compounds. A single meaningful journey can shift worldview, reset habits, influence life decisions, and strengthen identity more powerfully than multiple superficial trips. For modern travelers navigating time pressures, economic realities, and environmental responsibility, mindset becomes the multiplier. Investing in presence yields the greatest returns - psychologically, socially, and ethically.

## Considerations for Travelers

To integrate the ideas in Part 2, consider:

- Let discomfort be purposeful. Seek challenges in safe, meaningful doses. Avoid defaulting to comfort bubbles.
- Prioritize depth over volume. Fewer destinations, deeper experience, richer learning.

- Travel as a global citizen, not a consumer. Awe is a doorway to responsibility, leave places and people better than you found them.
- Share the journey. Travel with partners, family, peers, shared experience accelerates trust, insight, and connection.
- Protect your attention. Put the phone down. Look longer. Listen deeper. Let reality arrive unfiltered.
- Return transformed. The true test of travel is not where you went, but how it changes how you live, lead, and relate when home.

In the next part of this book, we shift from what happens within the mind to how travelers navigate an ever-changing world. As the rules of exploration evolve in response to digital disruption, climate change, and shifting cultural landscapes, we ask: How can we travel more consciously, adaptively, and ethically in the face of new realities?

# PART 3

# The New Rules of Exploration

"We travel not to escape life, but for life not to escape us"

*Anonymous*

## THE NEW RULES OF EXPLORATION

Exploration has always involved risk, adaptation, and discovery. But in today's world, the landscape of exploration itself is shifting. Climate change is redrawing the physical map. Technology is transforming how we plan, experience, and share our journeys. Cultural and ethical awareness are reshaping how we move through space, how we connect with others, and how we define the purpose of travel.

In Part 3, we confront the evolving nature of exploration in the 21st century and ask what it means to be a responsible, conscious traveler in a world undergoing rapid transformation. This section focuses on how macro forces like digital acceleration, environmental urgency, global migration, and cultural interdependence are rewriting the travel experience.

The rise of digital nomadism and remote work has separated mobility from traditional structures, giving people the freedom to move, but also introducing questions about sustainability, belonging, and privilege. Artificial intelligence is reshaping decision-making, what we see, where we go, and how we engage with unfamiliar places, often automating what was once intuitive or serendipitous. Meanwhile, a renewed desire for authentic human connection has led travelers to seek out deeper, more intense experiences, shared meals, communal journeys, and cultural immersion that move beyond superficial interaction. These shifts require not just logistical adaptation, but cognitive and ethical evolution. The traveler of the future must learn to balance convenience with consciousness, freedom with responsibility, access with humility.

Exploration is no longer just about finding the new, it is about learning how to engage with complexity, how to adapt to rapidly changing contexts, and how to remain curious while also being respectful and informed. How to see a place a second or third time with fresh perspective and eagerness to learn something different.

As travel becomes increasingly curated, digitized, and designed for comfort, we face an emerging psychological tension: are we losing the ability to explore freely, take risks responsibly, and navigate the unknown? A growing cultural preference for predictability, resort-style travel, algorithm-directed itineraries, comfort-centric experiences risks dulling our adaptive instincts. True exploration requires stepping into uncertainty, exercising judgment, and embracing surprise. In a world engineered to reduce friction, we must actively preserve the capacities that travel once trained effortlessly: resilience, situational awareness, openness to the unpredictable, and the humility to meet differences without defensiveness. The future of exploration depends not only on where we can go, but on our willingness to experience places without controlling them.

This section also explores the invisible layers of travel: the impact of language; the subtle mechanics of cultural interpretation; and the power dynamics of global movement. It asks us to listen more closely, to think more critically, and to move through the world not just as visitors, but as collaborators in a shared future.

In Part 3, readers are invited to reconsider what it means to explore not just geographically, but ethically, technologically, and relationally. The new frontier is not only outer space or undiscovered terrain; it is our capacity to navigate uncertainty with purpose, to travel with humility, and to remain human in a world increasingly mediated by systems, screens, and algorithms.

# Digital Nomads and Remote Realities

In the past, travel and work existed in separate domains, one for leisure and the other for livelihood. Today, those lines are dissolving. The rise of remote work and digital connectivity has created a new archetype: the digital nomad. Equipped with laptops and Wi-Fi, individuals are increasingly choosing to live and work while on the move, trading traditional offices for coworking spaces in Bali, coffee shops in Lisbon, or cabins in the Andes. This chapter explores the emergence of this global mobility movement, its psychological and social dimensions, and the shifting definition of what it means to belong somewhere in an age of fluid geographies.

## THE NEW RULES OF EXPLORATION

Digital nomadism marks a shift in how people organize their lives, blending work, mobility, and identity in ways that challenge traditional models of stability and belonging. It reflects broader changes in how people view productivity, freedom, identity, and meaning. For many, location independence is not just a perk; it is a core value. The ability to choose one's environment is seen as an act of self-authorship, a rejection of rigid systems in favor of autonomy, exploration, and personal agency.

Psychologically, this mode of living alters how individuals relate to space, time, and social connection. Without a fixed address, the concept of home becomes fluid. Some nomads find freedom in this impermanence; others wrestle with the erosion of continuity and rootedness. The psychology of place attachment, the emotional bond between person and place is challenged in this context. Our sense of social identity is disrupted, and the need to evolve and incorporate our new surroundings into our identity is critical. While novelty can stimulate creativity and learning, it can also create a low-level sense of transience, reducing the depth of relationships and increasing feelings of dislocation.

The lifestyle of digital nomads engages several of the brain's adaptive systems. Regular exposure to new environments stimulates attentional networks, supporting greater neuroplasticity and cognitive flexibility. However, it may also contribute to decision fatigue and cognitive overload, especially when routines are absent or social systems are not well established. The brain thrives on a mix of novelty and stability. Without the latter, individuals may experience increased stress or emotional burnout, despite the perceived freedom.

Socially, digital nomadism redefines community. Traditional support systems, family, long-term friendships, neighborhood ties are often replaced by transient relationships and online networks. While this can foster global perspectives and diverse collaborations, it can also lead to relational fragmentation. Belonging becomes episodic. Connection, while frequent, may lack depth. Many nomads describe a paradox: being constantly surrounded by people, yet often feeling alone.

Economically and ethically, digital nomadism raises important questions. The ability to live affordably in countries with lower costs of living often relies on global economic disparity. Some nomads contribute meaningfully to local economies and communities; others exist in isolated bubbles of privilege. The influx of mobile workers can strain local infrastructure, inflate housing prices, and deepen inequality. This creates a growing need for what we might call ethical mobility, a conscious awareness of one's impact and a commitment to reciprocal, respectful engagement. The broader implications of this lifestyle also extend into identity.

Digital nomads often straddle multiple roles: tourist, worker, resident, outsider. This fluidity can be liberating, allowing for constant reinvention. But it can also create a kind of identity fatigue, a lack of clear belonging that complicates one's sense of self and social role. In psychological terms, the lack of stable reference points can disrupt narrative coherence, making it harder to construct a consistent personal story. At its best, digital nomadism offers a blueprint for rethinking how we work, live, and connect. It shows us that productivity is not location-bound, that cultural immersion can be ongoing, and that alternative lifestyles are possible. But it also reveals the need for structure, reflection, and intention.

The freedom to roam requires inner anchoring. Mobility without mindfulness can drift into rootlessness. Moving forward, cities and countries are beginning to adapt to this shift. Remote work visas, digital infrastructure, and mobile communities are being developed to support the growing number of people choosing this lifestyle. But infrastructure alone is not enough. We must also develop the psychological infrastructure, the mental and emotional skills to thrive in a world where location is optional but connection is essential.

So too is the obligation of digital nomads to role model global citizenship wherever they choose their base to be in that moment. Understanding and practicing cultural norms of their current home, attempting to integrate into communities beyond the nomad community. For communities where digital nomads reside, to create a welcoming space for them to integrate, to feel part of an ingroup, to leave the nomad with a message and respect for the people and place they have resided temporarily that can be shared and passed on to the next. We all have a role to play, as a digital nomad and as a community host.

At the same time, the rise of mobile lifestyles invites a deeper question of regenerative presence rather than passive occupation. The ability to live and work anywhere comes with a reciprocal duty: to contribute rather than simply extract lifestyle benefits. This means engaging in local economies beyond convenience spending, participating in civic rhythms rather than hovering on the edges, and ensuring our presence strengthens the social, cultural, and ecological fabric of the places we temporarily call home. When practiced consciously, digital nomadism can become a form of distributed cultural stewardship building bridges, transferring knowledge, and cultivating shared prosperity rather than amplifying inequality or displacement.

In the next chapter, we turn to the role of artificial intelligence in shaping travel choices. As algorithms increasingly mediate where we go, what we see, and how we experience, we ask: What is gained and what is lost when technology becomes our primary guide?

# AI Itineraries, Human Choice

In today's digital landscape, travel planning has become a highly mediated experience. With the rise of artificial intelligence, algorithms are no longer just assisting our decisions, they are actively shaping them. From personalized recommendations to real-time adjustments, AI now influences where we go, what we do, what we see, and even how we interpret what we encounter.

This chapter explores how algorithmic systems are redefining exploration, the psychological trade-offs involved, and the urgent need to preserve human agency in a world of machine-curated movement.

AI-powered platforms promise convenience. With a few taps, travelers can receive curated itineraries, optimized routes, tailored restaurant suggestions, and real-time translation assistance. Recommendation engines analyze user behavior, preferences, and past travel data to offer increasingly accurate suggestions. These tools can reduce friction, expand access, and open up new possibilities particularly for those new to a region or traveling on limited time. Yet the very features that make AI so effective also raise critical questions about autonomy, awareness, and experience.

At a psychological level, reliance on algorithms shifts how we relate to choice. When decisions are outsourced to technology, our capacity for independent exploration can diminish. This is known in cognitive science as automation bias, the tendency to over-trust decisions made by automated systems, even when they are flawed or misaligned with our values. Over time, this can erode our sense of agency, reducing decision-making to passive acceptance. What is lost is not just spontaneity, but the deeper self-reflection and growth that comes from navigating uncertainty on our own terms.

Outsourcing cognitive load may have mixed effects on the brain. While it can reduce decision fatigue and free up mental energy for deeper engagement, it may also limit the regular use of executive functions, skills essential for planning, self-regulation, and adaptability. Active engagement with our environment, including wayfinding, interpreting cultural cues, and choosing paths forward, stimulates the prefrontal cortex. If these processes are consistently bypassed, the richness of the learning experience may be diminished.

AI also influences what we see and what we don't. Recommendation systems are designed to surface what is most "relevant," "popular," or "similar" to previous choices. But this personalization often narrows rather than broadens experience. Known as the filter bubble effect, this algorithmic narrowing can limit exposure to diverse or unexpected encounters. A traveler might visit only the most rated restaurants or scenic viewpoints, while bypassing the quiet park, local gallery, or conversation with a stranger that might have offered a deeper connection. In this way, AI can reinforce a homogenized version of travel, even as it claims to personalize it.

There is also a subtle shift in narrative. Traditional travel involved interpretation deciding what something meant, what to prioritize, what to notice. Now, that interpretive work is increasingly done for us. AI-generated reviews, summaries, and suggested captions guide not just what we see, but how we frame our experiences. Over time, this can shape the story we tell about a place and about ourselves. The danger is not that technology provides support, but that it replaces the reflective processes that help us grow. AI in essence can deteriorate our curiosity by stealth. However, the integration of AI into travel is not inherently negative. These systems can enhance safety, reduce stress, and democratize access. Used wisely, they can empower travelers to go farther, deeper, and with more context than ever before.

The challenge is to remain conscious of how we use these tools. Are we augmenting our experience or replacing it? Are we using technology to deepen understanding or to avoid discomfort and complexity?

The ethical dimensions of AI in travel are equally important. Algorithmic systems reflect the biases of their creators and the limitations of their datasets. This can result in unequal representation of destinations, cultural misinterpretations, or the amplification of certain narratives over others. In regions underrepresented in digital content, AI may fail to offer useful guidance altogether, reinforcing global imbalances. Culturally sensitive travel requires more than data, it requires intention, context, and humility.

Ultimately, the future of exploration will involve a partnership between human insight and machine intelligence. But that partnership must be designed with care. AI can offer paths but it is up to us to choose which to follow. It can suggest but not feel; it can optimize, but not wonder. It cannot replace the inner work of curiosity, reflection, and growth. These are uniquely human capacities, and they are at the heart of meaningful travel.

The opportunity ahead is not to reject technology, but to wield it with discernment, to use AI as a compass rather than a cage. Conscious travelers will increasingly cultivate hybrid navigation: algorithm-assisted exploration balanced with intuition, curiosity, and situational awareness. In this model, technology becomes a tool for empowerment, not dependency. We preserve serendipity by leaving open space in the itinerary; we strengthen personal agency by making decisions the algorithm cannot predict; we protect creative and cognitive vitality by choosing presence over passive automation. In the future of travel, mental sovereignty, the ability to think, choose, and explore autonomously becomes both a skill and a privilege worth protecting. Take time to reflect on how you might use technology to travel consciously, if you've done so in the past, or plan to do so in the future.

In the next chapter, we explore the relational dimensions of the journey. As technology continues to mediate travel, what does it mean to connect truly and intensely with others? How do shared experiences shape memory, belonging, and emotional resonance in a world of increasing fragmentation?

# Connection, Intensity and the Shared Journey

Some of the most enduring travel memories are not about places, but about people, those we travel with, those we meet along the way, and those with whom we share the journey, even briefly. In an era defined by virtual interaction and digital convenience, the shared journey remains one of travel's most powerful and irreplaceable dimensions.

## THE NEW RULES OF EXPLORATION

This chapter explores how meaningful connection, especially when forged under novel or intense conditions, deepens emotional experience, enhances memory, and fosters belonging in an increasingly fragmented world.

Travel often compresses time and heightens emotion. This creates a psychological intensity that accelerates bonding. Whether navigating a foreign city, hiking through unfamiliar terrain, or sharing a meal with strangers, the context of travel strips away the formalities and routines of daily life. In this stripped-down space, connection can be fast and deep. Social psychologists describe this as accelerated intimacy, the phenomenon by which people form close relationships quickly when placed in new or emotionally heightened settings. The novelty of the environment acts as a catalyst, lowering defenses and opening space for more authentic interaction.

Shared experiences activate the brain's social and emotional systems. During moments of vulnerability, mutual effort, or emotional connection, oxytocin, the hormone linked to bonding and trust is released, reinforcing a sense of connection. At the same time, the mirror neuron system, which enables empathy and social understanding, is more likely to be engaged when we are co-experiencing unfamiliar stimuli. These systems together reinforce the sense of trust, familiarity, and connection that can emerge during shared travel. Importantly, the context of shared exploration allows people to connect not just through dialogue, but through action.

Problem-solving, navigating uncertainty, and co-creating moments in real time lead to what psychologists call co-regulation, a process by which people manage emotional states together. This is especially evident in group travel or communal experiences such as retreats, service projects, or pilgrimages. These moments foster a unique kind of relationship situated outside daily life, yet deeply embedded in memory and meaning.

From a cognitive perspective, shared experiences are more likely to be remembered vividly and positively. The "social glue" theory of memory suggests that emotions and social context enhance the consolidation of experience into long-term memory. When we reflect on our most meaningful travel moments, they are often tied to the presence of others, laughing together, getting lost, helping one another through discomfort. These shared narratives not only enrich our personal memories; they also become part of our relational fabric. Connection through travel is not limited to companions we know. Encounters with strangers, brief, unrepeatable, and often spontaneous, can also be profoundly meaningful. These encounters bypass the layers of identity we usually carry and allow for raw, human connection. They remind us that intimacy does not always require history; sometimes it simply requires presence, openness, and shared humanity. In the sociology of travel, such interactions are often referred to as "fleeting intimacies", powerful connections formed in transient circumstances, which, though brief, can have lasting emotional impact. However, connection in travel also carries complexity.

Cultural misunderstanding, language barriers, and differing norms can lead to miscommunication or distance. Moreover, not all travel experiences are designed for depth. Mass tourism, over-scheduled itineraries and highly mediated group trips can inhibit spontaneity and authentic connection. In these contexts, connection becomes performative, something constructed for the sake of social media or status, rather than for mutual understanding. To foster genuine connection, what matters most is being deliberate in how we show up. This means approaching others with curiosity rather than assumption, listening without expectation, and allowing space for discomfort and difference. It also means recognizing the relational ethics of travel being aware of the dynamics of privilege, power, and representation in cross-cultural engagement.

True connection is not about consumption or entertainment; it is about reciprocity and mutual regard. As technology increasingly mediates our interactions through translation apps, digital reviews, and curated experiences, it becomes even more vital to preserve space for unstructured human connection. Algorithms can guide us to places, but they cannot replicate the spontaneous laughter of a shared discovery or the vulnerability of getting lost together. These moments do not scale, and they do not need to. Their power lies precisely in their unrepeatable, human texture.

In a time when loneliness is rising and community is fraying, the shared journey matters more than ever. Travel offers a unique opportunity to reconnect not just with the world, but with each other. Shared travel also represents one of the most overlooked forms of leadership development and relational intelligence. When people navigate unfamiliar environments together, they reveal communication patterns, emotional tendencies, and values more quickly than in routine settings. Families strengthen trust and adaptability; leadership groups build cohesion and humility; romantic partners learn patience and co-regulation; friends turn into lifelong anchors through moments of challenge and awe. At a time where mediated interaction often replaces embodied experience, intentional shared travel becomes an antidote building social resilience, emotional fluency, and the ability to collaborate under uncertainty. In moments of mutual presence, shared wonder, and co-created meaning, we find reminders of what binds us, even across vast differences.

In the next chapter, we examine how language, culture, and humility shape our experience of the world. What does it mean to listen well, to step into another's frame of reference, and to travel not only with awareness, but with reverence?

# Language, Culture and Humility

To travel across borders is to enter someone else's narrative. Every culture has its own rhythm, its own logic, its own set of expectations about how life unfolds. For the traveler, stepping into this space demands more than observation, it calls for humility.

In this chapter, we examine how language and culture shape our experience of the world, and why humility is not just a virtue but a necessary skill for meaningful exploration.

Language is more than a tool for communication; it contains social cues and priorities that often remain invisible to the speaker but become obvious when highlighting the differences between languages. These embedded patterns don't exist in isolation; they interact with broader cultural frameworks. Cultural Dimensions Theory, developed by Geert Hofstede, helps explain these shared patterns by mapping how societies differ in areas such as individualism, power distance, uncertainty avoidance, and time orientation.

## CULTURAL DIMENSIONS THEORY

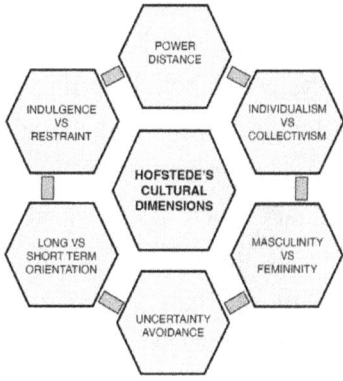

The structure of a language influences how its speakers perceive time, emotion, relationships, and even space. For instance, some languages use absolute directions (north, south) rather than relative ones (left, right), which leads to a more developed spatial orientation. Others assign gender to inanimate objects, which can subtly influence perception and behavior. Linguists call this the linguistic relativity hypothesis, the idea that language shapes thought.

When we travel and engage with unfamiliar languages, we are not just translating words; we are translating frameworks of meaning. Attempting to learn or speak another language, even imperfectly, is a powerful act of respect. It signals a willingness to step outside one's own comfort zone and engage with the world on someone else's terms.

Engaging in this kind of learning activates multiple brain systems, including those involved in memory, empathy, and problem-solving. Acquiring a new language builds cognitive flexibility and sharpens sensitivity to nuance not only in vocabulary, but in tone, behavior, and cultural context. But humility in travel is about more than language. It is about acknowledging that our way is not the only way, and that our perspective is shaped by culture as much as anyone else's.

Cultural humility involves the ongoing process of self-reflection and learning, particularly in the face of difference. It is not the same as cultural competence, which can sometimes suggest mastery. Rather, cultural humility begins with the assumption that we do not and cannot know everything. It invites curiosity, patience, and openness to correction. It shifts our mind into growth mindset mode, where every opportunity is seen as learning. Psychologically, humility reduces defensiveness and increases the capacity for learning. It quiets the ego, allowing new information to be integrated without immediate judgment. This state of mind is essential in travel, where things often don't go as planned, and where assumptions can quickly lead to misunderstanding. This state of mind makes us more resilient to changing circumstances.

Cognitive science shows that when we approach a situation with intellectual humility, we are more likely to update our beliefs, consider alternative viewpoints, and experience emotional growth. Cross-cultural experiences provide fertile ground for developing this mindset. They often challenge deeply held assumptions about politeness, time, hospitality, or personal space. What is considered rude in one culture may be seen as respectful in another. What is efficient in one context may be seen as abrupt in another. These moments of tension are not failures of travel; they are its core lessons. They remind us that human norms are not universal, and that difference is not a deficiency.

Importantly, cultural humility also involves recognizing power dynamics. Travelers move with passports that grant varying levels of access, currencies that stretch differently, and identities that carry different privileges. Ethical travel requires awareness of these dynamics and a commitment to engaging with places and people in ways that are reciprocal, not extractive. This might mean choosing locally owned accommodations, supporting community-based tourism, or simply listening more than speaking.

In practice, cultural humility is enacted through small gestures: asking before taking photos, learning a few words in the local language, observing before participating, acknowledging when we don't understand. It's found in the pause before assuming, the question asked with genuine interest, the willingness to be uncomfortable. These acts not only deepen the travel experience; they build trust, respect, and shared humanity. In a world increasingly polarized by misunderstanding and cultural tension, travel offers a powerful counterforce if approached with humility. It reminds us that the world is vast, that people are endlessly complex, and that wisdom begins with listening. To travel humbly is to walk lightly, speak carefully, and pay close attention not just to what is different, but to what it reveals about ourselves.

Humility in travel is also the gateway to regeneration, not just learning from a place, but participating in its wellbeing. Regenerative travelers move beyond minimizing harm toward actively contributing: preserving cultural heritage rather than commodifying it, supporting biodiversity rather than burdening ecosystems, uplifting local knowledge rather than overshadowing it with imported assumptions. This mindset reframes travel from consumption to reciprocity, from arrival to participation, from passing through to leaving positive traces. When humility drives behavior, travel evolves into a practice of shared stewardship for the cultural and ecological commons that belong to all of us.

# The Psychology of Belonging Abroad

There is a particular moment familiar to many travelers, the instant you step into a new place and feel a subtle shift inside you. Not quite home, not entirely foreign. A sense of possibility, but also a quiet question "Where do I fit here?"

Belonging abroad is neither automatic, nor guaranteed. It is negotiated; earned; and felt in fragments before it becomes rooted. And while the physical act of travel often captures our cultural imagination, the psychological work beneath it, learning to belong somewhere new without possession, expectation, or entitlement, is one of its most transformative dimensions.

To belong abroad is to hold two truths simultaneously: that we are guests, and that we are capable of connection wherever humans gather.

Psychologists describe belonging as a fundamental human need, equal in importance to safety and food. Abroad, this need takes on new texture. Our familiar identity markers (i.e. profession, accent, routines) lose their anchoring power. Social roles become fluid. The cues that once helped us signal "who we are" fall away, and in their absence, we discover a more essential version of self.

Travel exposes us to the relational architecture of belonging. We learn that belonging is not delivered through geography, but through participation. Buying fruit at the neighborhood market each morning. Warmly greeting the café owner in the morning. Sitting in a local park long enough that a stranger becomes familiar. The rhythm of repeated presence makes us legible to others, and in that recognition, we begin to be held by place.

Belonging abroad also surfaces the psychology of identity expansion. Foreign environments ask us to adapt, to listen more than we speak, to observe before we conclude, to adopt humility as a posture rather than an intermittent practice. Over time, these micro-adaptations reshape self-perception. We become more porous, more layered, more capable of holding multiple cultural truths without fragmentation.

There is vulnerability in entering a context not designed around us. Loneliness, miscommunication, cultural friction, and the absence of anchors can be disorienting. But these moments are not failures of belonging, they are the curriculum. They deepen resilience, empathy, and perspective. They teach us that belonging is not comfort; it is participation in complexity.

True belonging abroad does not erase difference, it honors it. It invites us to show up not as spectators, but as respectful participants in the living story of a place. It asks us to be shaped, not just accommodated. It reminds us that belonging is not ownership, but a relationship.

And perhaps most importantly, belonging abroad changes how we belong at home. Returning, we notice what we once overlooked: the cadence of familiar streets, the unspoken cultural rituals we had taken for granted, the people and places that shape our sense of self. The world outside gives us back the world inside with sharper clarity. In learning to belong elsewhere, we learn to belong more consciously everywhere.

# Travel and Power - Privilege, Access, and Equity

To cross borders is never simply a logistical act. It is a negotiation of power, visible and invisible, historical and contemporary. Every passport stamp, every visa waiver, every passage through customs is shaped by structures far larger than the individual holding the documents.

Travel feels personal, but it exists inside systems: geopolitical histories, economic hierarchies, racial and cultural biases, inherited inequalities, and access shaped by chance as much as by choice.

## THE NEW RULES OF EXPLORATION

To explore the world is a privilege, and to pretend otherwise is to misunderstand the landscape we move through. When we recognize the unequal realities behind mobility, we travel with greater awareness and curiosity, and humility rather than entitlement.

Power travels with us. It shows up in the passport we carry. The currency we spend. The language we speak. The skin we wear. The stereotypes projected onto us or absent from us. For some, borders open like invitations. For others, they brace for questioning, surveillance, suspicion. One traveler moves through a security line with ease; another prepares their narrative in advance, rehearsing legitimacy.

The right to movement is not evenly distributed and it never has been. This imbalance is not only geopolitical, it is psychological. Travel can reinforce hierarchy: the "insider" and the "visitor," the "global citizen" and the "local," the "observer" and the "observed". When movement becomes extraction of culture, of imagery, of labor, of environment, it echoes older systems of power.

But travel can also interrupt these patterns. It can become a practice of recognition rather than consumption. A way of seeing power instead of benefiting from its invisibility.

To travel consciously is to ask:

- Who cannot move where I move?
- Who prepares my arrival behind the scenes?
- Whose culture am I entering, and what histories does it hold?
- What narratives do I carry with me, and which ones do I inherit?
- Am I entering as a learner or as a consumer?

These questions do not diminish the joy of travel, they deepen it. They turn moments of privilege into moments of responsibility and reciprocity. They remind us that we are guests, never owners of other people's stories or spaces.

Inequity in travel is an undeniable reality. Acknowledging it is the first step, inviting awareness, responsibility, and a willingness to notice who is included, who is excluded, and who bears the impact. While travel opens us, it can also blind us if we do not look beyond the postcard horizon.

The next era of movement will belong to travelers who can hold dual truths: joy and responsibility, wonder and awareness, freedom and accountability. To move well in the world is not to take lightly the privilege of movement, but to carry it with intention, to travel gently, gratefully, and in solidarity with those whose worlds are shaped by borders they cannot cross.

When travel becomes not just access, but agency used with care, it shifts from entitlement to stewardship. It becomes not only a personal experience, but a shared ethical act. In that shift, movement becomes more powerful, not less.

With this, we conclude Part 3 and prepare to move inward. In the next section, we explore the internal dimension of exploration, the mindset that emerges not just from movement through the world, but from reflection, integration, and the ongoing journey of becoming.

## Considerations for Travelers

To integrate the ideas in Part 3, consider:

- Build your tolerance for the unknown. Lean into manageable uncertainty. Over-managed experiences don't make us stronger; they make us dependent.

## MINDSET FOR THE FUTURE

- Use technology, don't let it use you. Let algorithms inform, not govern. Leave room for wonder, mistakes, and discovery.
- Be a regenerative presence. Leave places, ecosystems, and communities better than you found them, materially and relationally.
- Travel as a true guest, not a consumer. Learn norms, practice language, seek context, honor local rhythms.
- Build shared memory. Travel with people who matter. Invest in collective experience, it compounds trust and emotional depth.
- Anchor through inner stability. External mobility requires internal grounding, such as routines, reflection, purpose.
- Stay curious, stay human. Adaptation, humility, and real connection are the modern explorer's core competencies.

# PART 4

# Becoming a Conscious Explorer

"The joy of life comes from our encounters with new experiences, and hence there is no greater joy than to have an endlessly changing horizon."

- *Christopher McCandless*

Every journey has an outer path and an inner one. While the literal itinerary may include planes, trains, and border crossings, deeper movement often happens beneath the surface, in the shifts of mindset.

Part 4 turns inward, exploring what it means to become a conscious explorer: someone who travels not just to see the world, but to see themselves more clearly through it. This section moves beyond destinations to focus on awareness. What internal capacities make us better travelers, and how do our outer experiences shape inner transformation?

Across cultures and disciplines, the idea of travel as pilgrimage, and as a form of personal evolution, is as old as human movement itself. In the modern world, where travel is more accessible and fast-paced, we must ask: How do we ensure the lessons of the road are not lost in motion? How do we pause long enough to integrate what we encounter? At the center of this inquiry is mindset. To be a conscious traveler is to engage intentionally with one's surroundings, reactions, and inner dialogue. It means noticing not just where we are, but how we are. It requires the ability to listen deeply and without interruption, to people, to places, and to oneself. In a world that prizes movement, presence becomes a radical act.

## BECOMING A CONSCIOUS EXPLORER

In the following chapters, we explore practices that support this inner journey. We examine the power of listening as a travel skill, not only in conversation but in attention to silence, emotion, and story. We look at what it means to come home changed, and how to carry forward the insights gained abroad into everyday life. Finally, we reframe travel itself as a state of mind, one defined less by physical distance and more by perspective, reflection, and openness to growth.

Becoming a conscious explorer is a journey in cultivating the ability to live inside questions, to tolerate ambiguity, and to remain receptive to transformation. It is about moving through the world not with certainty, but with curiosity and care.

A conscious explorer also treats inner work as a practical discipline with tangible returns as our own social identity evolves: clearer decision-making, steadier emotions under pressure, richer relationships on the road, and far more durable memories. When presence deepens, the return on investment of every mile rises. Instead of rushing after the next experience, we absorb the one in front of us. This mindset compounds over time: the more we train attention and humility, the more each journey pays dividends in well-being, wisdom, and the capacity to contribute.

# The Mindset of Listening

In the age of constant broadcast, where opinions are shared instantly and platforms reward speed over depth, the skill of listening has never been more endangered, or more essential. For the conscious traveler, listening is not a passive act. It is a mindset and a cultivated, intentional approach to engaging with the world, that begins with curiosity, requires presence, and honors complexity.

## BECOMING A CONSCIOUS EXPLORER

In this chapter, we explore listening as a transformative travel practice. It's a way to understand others, attune to context, and deepen personal insight. Our individual perception of reality is flawed. It's only when we listen to others that true reality emerges.

Listening in travel extends beyond conversation. It includes paying attention to gesture, tone, silence, environment, and cultural nuance. It means noticing what is not said, sensing the atmosphere of a place, and being present enough to allow meaning to emerge on its own terms. This form of listening is rooted in embodied cognition, the psychological understanding that perception is not just mental, but physical and emotional. We listen with our bodies, with our nervous systems, with the posture of our presence.

When we travel, much of what we learn comes from observation. Long before we speak the language or understand the customs, we watch how people move, interact, and signal meaning. Social Learning Theory helps explain this process by showing how attention, memory, and motivation shape the way we absorb behaviors in unfamiliar environments. For example, a traveler in Japan may quickly notice how quietly people board public transport and instinctively mirror that behavior, not because it was explained, but because it was observed, retained, and reproduced.

## SOCIAL LEARNING THEORY

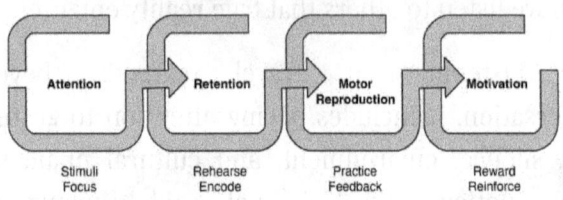

Deep listening engages brain networks involved in empathy, memory, and executive function. Regions such as the temporo-parietal junction (TPJ) and anterior insula, linked to perspective-taking and emotional resonance are especially active when we are fully present with another person's experience. Listening quiets the brain's default narrative mode and shifts attention outward, creating space for understanding that is less filtered by assumption and more attuned to the speaker.

In cross-cultural contexts, this capacity becomes even more vital. Language barriers, social norms, and unfamiliar contexts can make communication fragile. When we rely on speaking or interpreting alone, misunderstanding is almost inevitable. But when we lead with listening, suspending judgment and attuning to context, we allow for a more reciprocal and respectful exchange. Cultural anthropologists often describe this as "participant observation", the act of learning through humility, presence, and observation rather than imposition. Listening is also a key pathway to empathy.

Empathy in travel is not simply about feeling what another feels; it is about recognizing the legitimacy of their experience. It is about accepting that every story we encounter is shaped by forces we may not fully understand, including valuable historical contexts. To listen in this way is to acknowledge that we do not enter neutral spaces. We enter as guests, as learners, and sometimes as representatives of complex systems. The conscious traveler listens with this awareness.

At a psychological level, listening also strengthens metacognition, which is our ability to reflect on our own thinking. When we listen to others, we are often confronted with different assumptions, different logics, and different ways of seeing the world. These moments of contrast prompt internal inquiry: Why do I think this way? Where did this belief come from? What might I be missing? In this way, listening becomes a tool for inner alignment. It sharpens self-awareness and deepens personal growth. Practicing the mindset of listening requires intention. It may involve slowing down, asking fewer questions, and allowing silence to stretch beyond what is comfortable. It may mean staying curious when we feel defensive, or withholding interpretation until more context is known. These micro-moments of restraint are not weakness; they are the discipline of presence. They allow for richer understanding, more authentic relationships, and fewer assumptions.

Importantly, listening does not mean agreement or passivity. It means making space. Holding ambiguity. Allowing another to be fully seen and heard without needing to fix, compare, or control. In travel, this might look like sitting in a marketplace without a camera, attending a religious service without commentary, or listening to someone's story without inserting our own. These acts are subtle, but they are profound. They tell the world "I am here and I am willing to learn". In a fragmented world, listening is an act of connection. It is a way to cross boundaries without erasing differences. It invites depth in a culture of surface, and it cultivates peace in a climate of noise. For the traveler, it is both method and mindset, one that expands understanding and, over time, changes how we move through the world.

In the next chapter, we explore what happens after the journey ends. How do we return home changed? How do we carry forward the insights gained on the road? And what does it mean to integrate travel not just into memory, but into the ongoing story of who we are becoming?

Listening also regenerates the social ecosystems we enter. When we lead with attention rather than assertion, we reduce friction, honor context, and create moments to build trust by sending small, human signals even in situations fatigued by hurried tourism. Practically, this looks like learning names, asking consent, inviting local voices to author the narrative, and letting silence breathe. Over time, these choices shift travel from extraction to reciprocity, leaving relationships stronger than we found them.

# Coming Home Changed - The Neuroscience of Memories & Experiences

Every journey ends in a return. But returning is not the same as going back. For those who have traveled with attention, openness, and reflection, the return home is often one of the most complex parts of the experience. It is a moment of transition between movement and stillness, between expansion and re-entry, between the person who left and the person who now returns.

## BECOMING A CONSCIOUS EXPLORER

In this chapter, we explore what it means to come home changed, and how to integrate the growth, insights, and disorientation that often follow meaningful travel.

The re-entry process is often underestimated. While much attention is given to preparing for departure, far less is given to the psychological and emotional terrain of returning. Yet many travelers report feelings of restlessness, disconnection, or even grief upon coming home. These are not signs of failure or dissatisfaction; they are indicators that transformation has occurred. The internal map no longer matches the external landscape. What once felt normal may now seem constricting. What was once overlooked now carries weight.

From a psychological perspective, this is a classic case of liminality, the state of being between identities, no longer who we were, not yet who we will become. Travel, especially when immersive or prolonged, acts as a liminal experience. It removes us from the known and immerses us in unfamiliarity, where our roles, routines, and assumptions are suspended. Upon return, we are asked to re-integrate; to reconcile the person we've become with the context we once inhabited. This is not always seamless.

Travel experiences that involve novelty, emotion, and reflection are more likely to form lasting memories because the brain encodes them more deeply. These changes are physiological. Networks involved in self-reflection and emotional relevance, including the default mode network and the salience network, reorganize when we encounter new environments and perspectives. When we return to familiar settings, these new patterns may not fit easily with our existing habits or beliefs, creating tension as the brain works to reconcile them. This process matters: it is how travel memories become meaningful in daily life, informing our decisions, shaping our viewpoints, and influencing how we respond to future situations.

The key to navigating this dissonance lies in integration. Integration is the process by which new experiences are translated into enduring understanding. It requires intentional reflection: What did I learn? How did I change? What matters more (or less) than it did before?

This reflection can take many forms: journaling, conversation, solitude, art, or community dialogue. Without integration, the insights of travel remain fragmented. Integration also means paying attention to how we re-engage with our environments. Are we able to bring back new practices, such as slowness, gratitude, presence, new recipes, or do we revert to old patterns out of habit or convenience? This tension is natural. Lasting change is rarely immediate. But by holding on to even one new habit or perspective, we affirm the value of our journey.

There is also a social dimension to coming home changed. Sharing our experiences with others is part of the integration process, but it requires discernment. Not everyone will understand or relate to what we've seen or felt. Some will be interested; others may be indifferent or even resistant. Here, the challenge is to avoid performance, reducing complex experiences into highlight reels or moral lessons, and instead offer stories that invite connection and curiosity.

Listening becomes just as important in return as it was while traveling. For those who travel regularly, this cycle of departure and return becomes part of the rhythm of life. But each return still presents an opportunity: to recalibrate priorities, to reimagine what 'home' means, to bring fresh energy into familiar spaces. In this sense, coming home is not a reversal, it is a new phase. The world has not changed, but we have. And in our changed perspective, new possibilities emerge.

The philosopher Martin Buber wrote, "All journeys have secret destinations of which the traveler is unaware." Often, one of those destinations is the self, an inner place we arrive at only after the outer journey has unfolded. Coming home changed means recognizing that we have touched that place, however briefly, and allowing it to inform how we move forward. In the final chapter of this section, we look at what happens when travel is no longer defined by movement. What if the mindset of the traveler (curious, open, adaptive) could be carried into everyday life? What if travel became less about geography and more about how we see?

Integration is where courage replaces performance. It asks us to trade the comfort of highlight reels for the discipline of how we adapt our behaviors e.g. modifying how we spend, how we schedule time, how we speak about other cultures at home, how we host travelers in our own city. Treat re-entry like a design sprint, distill learning, translate it into behaviors, and test them over time. The real measure of a journey is not what we posted while away, but what we practice when we return.

# Travel as a State of Mind

What if travel was never about geography alone? What if the essence of exploration (the curiosity, attention, and transformation it fosters) could be accessed without crossing borders?

In this final chapter of Part 4, we examine the idea that travel, at its most powerful, is less about place and more about perspective. That the mindset cultivated through meaningful travel, one of openness, wonder, and engagement, can become a way of being in the world, wherever we are.

At the heart of this idea is mental mobility: the ability to step outside our default patterns of thought and perception, to disrupt routine assumptions, and to see the familiar with new eyes. This is the internal equivalent of navigating a new city, entering an unfamiliar culture or completing a new walking track close to home. It's what cognitive scientists call cognitive flexibility, the capacity to shift perspectives, adapt to changing information, and respond creatively to uncertainty. It is a skill that can be practiced, whether or not we are physically moving. Travel helps cultivate this flexibility by forcing us to confront the unexpected. But with intention, the same mental shift can occur at home. It might come from entering a different part of one's own city, engaging deeply with someone from another background, or learning something that challenges long-held beliefs.

These micro-journeys activate the same neural systems associated with novelty, attention, and emotional salience, especially when we approach them with curiosity and presence. This reframing of travel is especially important in a world where movement is increasingly constrained by environmental, political, or economic forces. Not everyone can travel freely. Not every moment is one of outward expansion. But the capacity for inward exploration, the ability to notice, to inquire, to imagine, remains available to all. This democratizes the spirit of travel. It makes growth possible not just through distance, but through depth.

Adopting travel as a state of mind has been linked to greater resilience and well-being. Research shows that novelty and curiosity are closely associated with positive emotional states and long-term mental health. When we engage the world as if it were unfamiliar (even the parts we think we know) we invite fresh insight and renewed attention. This is what mindfulness researcher Ellen Langer refers to as "the psychology of possibility", the practice of noticing variability, embracing change, and staying alive to context. This mindset also redefines what we consider meaningful.

In traditional tourism, significance is often linked to distance, cost, or spectacle. But in a mindset-based model, meaning arises from awareness and intention. A conversation at a bus stop, a walk through a neighborhood park, or a quiet moment of reflection can be as transformational as a faraway adventure, if we're paying attention. The extraordinary becomes accessible through the quality of our presence. To live as a conscious explorer means cultivating this presence daily. It means seeing our own lives as terrains worth mapping. Our habits, relationships, thoughts, and assumptions become sites of inquiry. What do I take for granted? What patterns am I repeating? Where am I being called to change? This is inner travel, and it requires just as much courage, curiosity, and commitment as a trip abroad.

Importantly, this mindset is not about replacing physical travel, it's about extending its value. When we carry the traveler's mindset into daily life, we increase the return on every journey. The insights gained on the road become not just memories, but practices. They shape how we work, love, create, and respond to the world. They make life itself more vivid, more connected, more alive.

In closing Part 4, we invite readers to ask not just where they want to go, but how they want to be. What would it mean to bring the full presence of the traveler into each day? To listen with curiosity, to walk with wonder, to respond with humility? This is the mindset of the future, one that sees life itself as a journey, and each moment as a place to begin again.

With this perspective in place, we now move to the final part of the book: a practical examination of how travel can be reimagined, for individuals, industries, and institutions, in ways that are sustainable, ethical, and future-ready?

## BECOMING A CONSCIOUS EXPLORER

Cultivating "travel as a state of mind" also counters our era's comfort addiction. When life is over-designed for control (think of resorts, packaged certainty, algorithmic sameness) our social and cognitive muscles atrophy. To rebuild them, engineer small doses of healthy risk. Leave unplanned windows in your day, choose unscripted conversations over perfect ratings, take the slower route and notice. These micro-adventures protect adaptability, curiosity, and courage, the very capacities that make outer journeys meaningful when they do arrive.

# Travel and Well-being

Travel has long been romanticized as an antidote to stress, a reset button, a path to joy and renewal. Yet well-being in travel is not guaranteed by distance, scenery, or escape. It is shaped by intention, mindset, and the inner landscape we bring with us. Movement alone does not heal. What heals is how we move.

We travel not only to see the world, but to feel differently within it. To breathe more deeply. To remember spaciousness. To quiet the noise of routine long enough to hear ourselves again. And yet the modern traveler often arrives carrying the very burdens they sought relief from: urgency, comparison, distraction, self-optimization disguised as rest. A trip becomes another task. Rest becomes performance. Presence becomes content.

Well-being in travel begins before the journey. It begins in the decision to leave not as escape from life, but as reconnection to it.

Research in positive psychology shows that novelty, awe, and purposeful breaks in routine activate neural pathways associated with emotional resilience and cognitive flexibility. When we encounter unfamiliar environments, our attention widens. Our nervous system resets. Our sense of time stretches. These experiences don't simply give us a "break", they recalibrate us.

Yet peace is not found only in panoramic views or remote retreats. It is found in the way we receive them.

Slowness is medicine.
Attention is medicine.
Awe is medicine.

But they require space, internal as much as external.

Travel can soothe us, but it can also expose what we avoid. When the schedule clears, emotions surface. When identity is removed from familiar roles, confusion can arise. When silence replaces noise, restlessness appears. These moments often signal that something important is asking for attention. Travel gives us enough distance from our routines to notice what we usually overlook and to understand our inner landscape with more clarity.

The nervous system responds powerfully to place. We know this intuitively when a quiet shoreline softens our breath or a mountain horizon widens our chest. But connection is not passive, we must meet the landscape with presence. A walk without headphones. A meal without a photograph. A morning without a rushing plan.

And true rest is not cessation, it's replenishment.

Connection, not withdrawal.
Meaning, not escape.

## BECOMING A CONSCIOUS EXPLORER

The healthiest travel is not always the most glamorous. It is the journey where we slept enough, listened more, pushed less, felt ourselves more deeply, and allowed the world to soften us rather than stimulate us endlessly.

Well-being also lives in boundaries. Saying no to over-scheduling, constantly posting and to the myth that seeing more means feeling more. It lives in honoring our emotional needs in unfamiliar places, seeking solitude when we are saturated, connection when we feel untethered, and stillness when our nervous system asks for pause.

To travel for well-being is not to chase perfect moments, but to create conditions for honest ones. It is to let destinations inspire, not rescue. And to remember that the most restorative part of travel is not the distance from home, it's the closeness to self.

In this way, travel becomes not a temporary state of relief but a practice of renewal. A way of remembering how to breathe, how to feel, how to be human in a world that often asks us to hurry past ourselves.

The journey ends, but the well-being continues. The goal is to return not only rested, but rearranged. Not only soothed, but more awake to what sustains us. The greatest gift of movement is not escape, but to return to our lives with more clarity and more capacity to live fully where we are.

# The Loneliness & Connection Paradox

Travel promises connection. We imagine shared tables, chance friendships, oceanside conversations with strangers who feel instantly familiar. And often, this happens. Yet alongside the possibility of deep connection lies a quieter, often unspoken truth: travel can also be profoundly lonely.

The paradox is simple: When we are most surrounded by new faces, we may feel most aware of our aloneness.

Movement strips away familiarity, social roles, routine validation, the ease of being known without explanation. In this space, connection does not come automatically; it must be built. And before connection can emerge, loneliness often arrives first.

Loneliness while traveling is not a flaw in the experience, it is part of its emotional architecture.
It is the moment before belonging.
The pause before resonance.
The clearing before encounter.

Psychologically, novelty heightens emotional sensitivity. When everything is unfamiliar, the nervous system shifts into alertness, searching for safety and social cues. In these heightened states, the absence of close connection is felt more sharply. The brain, wired for belonging, scans for anchors. When none appears immediately, it can interpret isolation as threat, not freedom.

Yet loneliness can also prime us for connection in a way comfort rarely does. Stripped of habitual relationships, we become more present, more porous, more open to surprise. We listen differently. We seek differently. We notice details, a smile, a gesture, a shared inconvenience, the rhythm of local life.

Loneliness stretches us toward others, not away from them.

Travelers often describe fleeting yet profound moments of connection:
 a guide whose story reshapes a worldview,
 a hostel conversation that becomes confession,
 a long train ride shared in silence but deeply felt,
 a meal that dissolves cultural distance.

These connections are not accidental; they emerge from vulnerability. Neuroscience suggests that transient shared experiences can activate trust and empathy circuits when individuals are equally exposed to uncertainty. In travel, shared context accelerates intimacy. Strangers become companions faster than life at home allows, not because proximity guarantees intimacy, but because openness does.

There is also a cultural dimension. Some societies externalize hospitality naturally; others guard privacy. The traveler must learn to read these signals, to adapt without demanding familiarity on their terms. Connection must be invited, not extracted.

Importantly, loneliness is not always a condition to solve. It can be a teacher.

It reveals what (and who) we miss.
It clarifies what connection means beyond geography.
It reminds us that belonging is not only external; it is also internal.

But the paradox deepens in the digital age. Hyper-connectivity means we can FaceTime across oceans, yet such connections may soothe in the moment while preventing us from anchoring where we are.

Digital proximity can dull the necessity of presence. The challenge becomes discerning when connection serves us, and when it shields us from the experience we came to find.

To travel consciously is to hold both truths:
We can feel lonely and not lost.
We can be alone and not abandoned.
We can seek connection without rushing it, and honor solitude without fearing it.

When we allow loneliness to soften rather than harden us, it becomes a doorway rather than a wall. Connection emerges not as escape from solitude but as expression of it. The traveler learns not to fill space, but to inhabit it, until the world steps forward in return.

In the end, the paradox is also the gift:
Travel makes us more aware of our longing for belonging, and in doing so, more capable of belonging wherever we go.

# Intercultural Competence - Expanding our capacity to understand

To travel well is not only to see differences, but to learn how to live gracefully alongside it. Intercultural competence is the inner skill set that allows us to move through unfamiliar cultural landscapes with empathy, curiosity, and adaptability. It is not about accumulating trivia or mastering etiquette; it is about developing the emotional, cognitive, and relational capacity to understand worlds beyond our own and to recognize the limits of our perspective.

## BECOMING A CONSCIOUS EXPLORER

At its core, intercultural competence begins with self-awareness. Before we can understand others, we must first understand the lenses through which we see our assumptions, our cultural conditioning, our biases, and our blind spots. We do not enter another culture as neutral observers; we bring our histories, habits, and inherited narratives with us. The conscious traveler learns to notice these influences not with judgment, but with humility. Every culture is a system that makes sense to the people who live within it. What feels intuitive to one person may feel baffling to another not because one way is superior, but because meaning is always contextual.

Psychologically, intercultural competence calls upon perspective-taking networks in the brain. These are the circuits that help us imagine another's experience and suspend automatic interpretations. It requires emotional regulation, the ability to sit in confusion or contradiction without rushing to closure. It cultivates cognitive flexibility and the willingness to update beliefs when new information arises. These are not passive traits; they are mental muscles that grow through exposure, reflection, and discomfort.

Cultural intelligence is not about fluency in every norm or tradition. It is the ability to approach new environments with curiosity rather than judgment, to listen before reacting, and to ask questions that invite understanding rather than confirmation. It is learning to shift communication styles, to notice power dynamics, and to interpret not only words but silence, gesture, pace, and context.

Intercultural competence deepens belonging, by allowing us to build bridges without demanding that the other side look like home. It teaches us that multiple truths can coexist, that meaning expands when we share it, and that understanding is not achieved through certainty, but through presence.

To travel with intercultural sensitivity is to move through the world as a learner rather than a judge. It is to recognize that every place has something to teach us, not only about others, but about ourselves. Culture does not only live in temples and marketplaces; it lives in us - through the ways we speak, relate, assume, and interpret. When we develop the capacity to see culture, we also develop the capacity to see ourselves with greater clarity.

Ultimately, intercultural competence is not a skill solely for travel; it is a skill for global life. In a world where borders are porous yet tensions are high, where identities intersect and narratives collide, the ability to listen across differences is essential. It prepares us not only to move through the world, but to help shape a world worth moving through.

# The Role of Storytelling - Meaning Beyond Sharing

We travel to see the world, but we also travel to make sense of it. One of the oldest ways humans make sense of experience is through story. Long before passports, itineraries, or social feeds, journeys lived on through spoken language, campfires, temples, community courtyards, dinner tables. Travel was not simply movement; it was transmission. Tales of distant horizons shaped imagination, identity, and collective understanding. To travel was to return with perspective and to offer it as a contribution.

Today, storytelling has become tangled with performance. The modern traveler documents, broadcasts, curates. True storytelling is not performance; it's the act of transforming experience into meaning rather than just memory into media.

When we tell a travel story, we reveal how we saw, not just what we saw. We talk through values, judgments, hopes, blind spots. And in that process, we shape the world we describe. Narrative is not neutral. It can deepen empathy or reinforce distance. It can give voice or erase. It can build bridges or borders. And a narrative helps us to reinforce what we've processed from our experience.

The psychology of narrative shows that stories don't just recall experiences, they organize them. Neural networks consolidate memory around meaning, emotion, and coherence. In crafting a narrative, we craft ourselves. We choose what mattered. We choose what to carry forward. We decide who we became because of what we encountered.

The conscious traveler asks:
What story am I telling, and why?
Who benefits from the way I tell it?
What truths am I amplifying, and what truths am I ignoring?

To share responsibly is to move slowly with our words. To honor context. To imagine how a story lands in the ears of those it is about. To resist turning people into scenery or culture into ornament. It means crediting local knowledge, naming power, and remembering that every place belongs first to itself, not to our interpretation.

When done with curiosity and reverence, storytelling becomes a form of bridge-building, expanding what others see possible, inviting empathy across borders, widening the circle of belonging.

We do not travel to accumulate stories; we travel to deepen them. To tell them in ways that remind us our lives are interwoven with others. To tell them in ways that leave dignity intact. To tell them in ways that nurture wonder rather than consume it.

In the end, the story of travel is not about the places we pass through. It is about the person we become, and the world we help imagine, because of how we choose to remember.

## Considerations for Travelers

To integrate the ideas in Part 4, consider:

- Practice micro-listening daily. Before you speak, name one detail you've noticed (tone, gesture, context). Let this guide your next question.
- Design your re-entry. On the flight home, choose three insights and translate them into one behavior each. Calendar the first thirty days.
- Swap performance for presence. Before posting, ask: Who does this serve? If the answer is validation, pause and journal instead.
- Schedule uncertainty. Keep 15–20% of any trip unplanned to preserve serendipity and flexibility.
- Leave places better. Learn names, tip fairly, source local, ask consent for photos, and share credit when you tell the story.
- Build shared experiences on purpose. Travel with a partner, family, or peer group around a shared question or theme; debrief nightly.
- Track your return on investment. Measure the trip by clarity gained, habits changed, and relationships strengthened, not by distances or likes.

# PART 5

# Considerations

"Travelling – it leaves you speechless, then turns you into a storyteller."

- *Ibn Battuta*

## CONSIDERATIONS

By now, we've journeyed through why we travel, how travel shapes the brain and self, how exploration is evolving in a digital and cultural sense, and how the most important journey may be internal. But travel does not happen in a vacuum. It is embedded in larger systems - economic, environmental, technological, political.

In this final section, we widen the lens to examine the broader landscape in which modern travel takes place, and the decisions we must make to ensure its sustainability, inclusivity, and continued relevance as a positive for individuals and societies at large.

We begin by turning attention to the traveler, not just as a seeker of experience but as an agent of impact. What should the future-ready traveler consider before departing, while moving, and upon returning? How do we move through the world with intention and awareness of our ecological footprint, cultural influence, and social presence? Ethical travel is no longer a fringe idea, it is essential to the future of movement.

We then take a look at the travel industry itself, which faces a pivotal moment. Global tourism has rebounded in scale, but not always in substance. Issues of over-tourism, labor exploitation, and extractive models of growth threaten the integrity of the experience and the well-being of the communities it touches. How can businesses reimagine travel not as volume-driven but as value-driven? What innovations (technological, experiential, relational) can align the industry with human and planetary needs? The role of corporations is also evolving. With the rise of remote work, global teams, and professional nomadism, organizations must rethink how they support mobility, cross-cultural engagement, and distributed presence. In this chapter, we explore how travel becomes a part of organizational culture, learning, and resilience, and what it means for leadership in a borderless world.

Finally, we close the book with a look toward the horizon: a practice of strategic foresight applied to the future of travel. Drawing from trends in neuroscience, climate science, artificial intelligence, and human behavior, we explore what might be next. How will the next generation move? What values will guide them? What will "exploration" mean when the world is both more accessible and more at risk?

Part 5 does not offer prescriptive answers, but instead presents questions and frameworks to guide decision-making for individuals and institutions. If movement is going to be meaningful, it must also be mindful. If the mindset of the traveler is to matter, it must be matched with action that honors the complexity of the world we explore.

In doing so, this section asks us to see movement not just as experience, but as participation, a shared responsibility in shaping the cultural, ecological, and emotional landscapes we touch. The future of travel belongs to those who move with reciprocity, depth, and intention. Travelers and leaders must understand that meaningful journeys expand not only our world, but our stewardship within it.

# Considerations for the Traveler

In an age where travel is more accessible, more visible, and more impactful than ever, the question is no longer simply where to go, but how to go. The conscious traveler of today must move with a deeper sense of awareness, of their impact, privilege, and responsibility.

This chapter explores the practical, ethical, and psychological considerations that shape responsible travel in the 21st century, offering a framework not just for movement, but for meaningful engagement.

CONSIDERATIONS

The first and perhaps most foundational consideration is intentionality. Why are we traveling? Is it to escape, to discover, to connect, to contribute? Clarifying intent before departure can transform the nature of a trip. It influences not only what we seek, but how we respond to what we find.

Research in behavioral psychology shows that setting intentional goals before an experience significantly shapes emotional response and memory formation. An intentional traveler is more likely to engage meaningfully, to notice more, and to reflect more deeply on their experience. It also provides 'guardrails' when we slip into wanting to see and do too much.

Next is the question of impact. Every journey has a footprint, whether it's ecological, economic, and cultural. Air travel contributes to carbon emissions. Tourist infrastructure can strain local resources. Economies dependent on tourism can be volatile and unequal. These truths don't mean we should stop traveling, but we need to travel smarter. Mindful consumption (i.e. choosing local food, supporting community-owned businesses, avoiding exploitative activities) can redistribute value more equitably and ethically. Tools like carbon offset programs, slow travel methods, and responsible accommodation choices are part of a broader recalibration toward sustainability. They can also inspire our curiosity.

The rise of agrotourism is a great example of this. When travelers spend time on working farms, vineyards, or rural cooperatives, the experience is a chance to understand how food is grown, how land is cared for, and how local economies function. Visiting a small olive farm in southern Italy or a coffee cooperative in Costa Rica lets travelers see the full cycle of production, meet the people whose labor sustains the region, and contribute directly to the local economy in a way mass tourism often overlooks. These experiences slow down the pace of travel, redirect money into community-led initiatives, and deepen appreciation for the landscapes that sustain us. Agrotourism shows how curiosity and responsibility can coexist: we learn, participate, and leave with a clearer sense of our relationship to place.

Cultural literacy matters in travel because it shapes how we understand and interact with the places we enter. It's the awareness of a community's history, norms, values, and lived realities, and the ability to navigate them with respect. Showing up with some understanding of where we are and who we're meeting is a fundamental part of responsible travel. Learning about local customs, power dynamics, history, and social context is a basic form of respect. Cultural humility, as discussed earlier, requires that we approach each place not as a backdrop for our personal narrative, but as a complex living environment with its own needs and dignity. This means resisting appropriation, questioning stereotypes, and avoiding spaces where travel itself may be causing harm. Tour operators can do so much to facilitate this with factsheets and tour information events.

A traveler must also consider emotional readiness. Travel often surfaces internal dynamics such as loneliness, anxiety, bias and expectation. Going somewhere new doesn't guarantee transformation unless we are willing to engage with the discomfort it can bring.

The most effective preparation for meaningful travel is a willingness to be changed by what we encounter. That means being open to awe, confusion, joy, and vulnerability along the way. These states, when embraced, become catalysts for growth. Digital awareness is another growing concern. The impulse to document, post, and share is now deeply embedded in how many people experience travel. But this practice can shift the purpose of travel from being present to being performative. Before sharing, we can ask: Is this for connection, or for validation? Am I honoring the place and people depicted, or am I centering myself in a way that distorts the reality?

Ethical storytelling, particularly across cultural lines, requires care, consent, and context. Time is also a consideration. The pace at which we travel affects the depth of our engagement. Rushed, surface-level tourism often reproduces stereotypes and transactional relationships. Slower travel (i.e. staying longer in fewer places, building relationships, allowing for downtime) can foster empathy and understanding. As attention becomes increasingly fractured in our daily lives, travel offers a rare opportunity to re-train our focus.

Lastly, the conscious traveler embraces the idea of reciprocity and regeneration. Travel should not only take, it should also give, and give in a way that leaves a place, it's people and ourselves better than before. This doesn't mean turning every trip into a service project or mission, but rather bringing an ethic of contribution. This could mean mentoring others, sharing resources responsibly, engaging in cultural exchange with respect, or returning home to apply what was learned in meaningful ways. Reciprocity closes the loop between experience and action. Ultimately, the future of travel depends on travelers who are willing to look inward as much as outward.

## CONSIDERATIONS

This chapter offers no fixed rules, only guideposts. To move through the world with care is to acknowledge our shared humanity and our shared responsibility for the world we inherit.

To travel consciously in the years ahead is to recognize that every journey leaves an imprint, internal and external. The question is no longer only "What will I gain from this place?" but also "What will I give?" Conscious travel invites depth over sampling, dialogue over display, humility over assumption. When we move with presence, we shift from consumption to connection, from passive witness to active steward. In this way, the journey expands beyond the itinerary and becomes a practice in belonging and responsibility.

In the next chapter, we turn to the travel industry itself: the systems, models, and values that must evolve to support a more ethical and regenerative approach to global movement.

# Considerations for the Travel Industry

The travel industry is one of the world's most dynamic and far-reaching ecosystems. It spans aviation, hospitality, technology, insurance, culture, labor, and infrastructure, touching nearly every facet of global society. Yet for all its reach, the industry now faces a reckoning. The post-pandemic rebound, the climate emergency, the digital transformation of tourism, and the rising demand for ethical engagement have created a new inflection point.

In this chapter, we examine what it means for the travel industry to evolve toward a model that is more regenerative, inclusive, and resilient.

## CONSIDERATIONS

The traditional model of travel was built for scale. Its success metrics are centered on volume, including arrivals, bookings, and nights stayed. As this model expanded, so did its externalities. Over-tourism has strained ecosystems, displaced communities, and altered the cultural fabric of many destinations. Carbon-intensive operations continue to contribute significantly to global emissions. Labor exploitation remains an endemic issue in many tourism-dependent economies. If the travel industry is to thrive in the long term, it must move beyond growth at any cost. This shift begins with redefining value. Rather than measuring success solely by economic output, forward-thinking industry leaders are starting to consider metrics like community well-being, environmental regeneration, and cultural preservation.

Stakeholder Theory offers a useful lens for this shift. It proposes that organizations have responsibilities not only to customers and shareholders, but to all groups affected by their decisions, including workers, local communities, suppliers, and the environment. In the context of travel, this means recognizing destinations, ecosystems, and cultural stewards as central stakeholders rather than peripheral concerns. Using this framework helps clarify what a regenerative travel model must value and who it must serve.

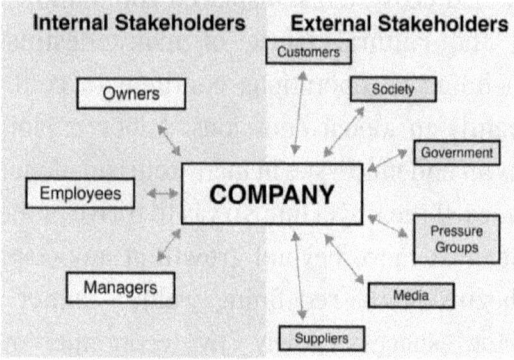

In practice, applying a stakeholder lens means making decisions that support all groups affected by travel, not just business profitability. Airlines exploring alternative fuels and route optimization. Hotels investing in energy efficiency and local supply chains. Tour operators partnering with Indigenous communities and offering immersive, respectful cultural experiences. These are steps towards a more accountable future.

Sustainability, though widely invoked, must become more than a marketing term. It must be operationalized through measurable standards,

## CONSIDERATIONS

transparent reporting, and authentic engagement. This means moving away from greenwashing and toward rigorous frameworks such as B Corp certification, carbon neutrality programs, and sustainable development goals (SDGs) integration.

Travelers are increasingly savvy; they can sense when values are performative rather than practiced. Another key consideration is inclusivity. Historically, much of the travel industry has catered to a narrow demographic: affluent, Western, able-bodied, and predominantly white. Reimagining travel means creating space for more diverse voices, as consumers, storytellers, creators, and decision-makers. This includes designing experiences that are accessible to all abilities, amplifying underrepresented cultures in marketing, and supporting businesses owned by women, Indigenous entrepreneurs, and historically marginalized communities. Travel should reflect the world it moves through.

Technology also plays a complex role in the future of travel. While digital platforms have increased access and personalization, they have also concentrated power in the hands of a few intermediaries. Booking algorithms, review systems, and digital surveillance can shape traveler behavior and destination visibility in ways that are opaque and biased. Ethical tech use in travel must prioritize transparency, user autonomy, and equitable representation. Innovations like AI-powered translation, virtual try-before-you-go tools, and regenerative booking engines hold promise, but only if designed with human values at the center.

Beyond systems and structures, the travel industry must also invest in emotional intelligence and mindset training for its workforce. From front-line hospitality to executive leadership, empathy, cultural literacy, and resilience are now critical competencies. The human element of travel cannot be replaced by automation. Experiences are shaped as much by interpersonal connection as by logistics. Training programs that foster perspective-taking, cross-cultural awareness, and emotional regulation are no longer optional, they are foundational.

Lastly, the industry must prepare for volatility. Climate disruption, political instability, and global health crises are not temporary anomalies, they are part of the new normal. This requires travel systems that are agile, decentralized, and capable of adapting without collapsing. Decentralized tourism models, where smaller, community-led enterprises create diverse and locally grounded offerings, may offer a blueprint for resilience. So too do regenerative principles, which move beyond sustainability to actively heal and restore the systems travel depends on.

The future of travel will not be shaped by a single innovation or policy, but by a shift in ethos. One that prioritizes purpose over volume, dignity over entertainment, and regeneration over extraction. The industry has the tools, talent, and influence to become a leader in global transformation. The question is whether it will have the will. In the next chapter, we explore the evolving role of travel within organizations. What does it mean for professionals and companies to think globally, move intentionally, and integrate travel into leadership, learning, and cultural strategy?

Leadership in travel will increasingly be judged by the impact it leaves behind. Growth for its own sake is losing relevance; what matters is whether a place is supported rather than depleted, and whether travelers return with a deeper sense of connection instead of disconnection. This shift is happening because of environmental limits, community fatigue with harmful tourism, and travelers' growing desire for meaning over consumption. In this context, care becomes the clearest indicator of good leadership. The industry's greatest opportunity is not to curate escape, but to cultivate understanding: designing journeys that regenerate ecosystems, honor local identity, and remind people of their shared place in a living world. Travel companies will become not just facilitators of movement, but custodians of meaning, cultural bridges, and guardians of place.

# Considerations for Corporate Explorers

Travel is not only a personal or recreational act, it's increasingly integral to the way organizations operate, collaborate, and grow. From remote work and cross-cultural teams to international leadership development and market expansion, corporate life now moves across borders with unprecedented fluidity.

In this chapter, we examine the evolving role of travel within professional life and organizational strategy, exploring how companies can approach mobility as a tool for learning, adaptability, and global competence.

The COVID-19 pandemic accelerated a trend already in motion: the decoupling of work from place. Today, distributed teams, virtual collaboration, and asynchronous operations are commonplace. Yet paradoxically, this decentralization has made the moments of physical connection (i.e. offsites, conferences, site visits, cultural immersions) more valuable than ever.

Travel is no longer just a logistical function of business. It is a space for collaboration, creativity, and cultural intelligence. For corporate travelers (professionals who move across regions to meet clients, build relationships, solve problems, or support teams) this shift opens new possibilities. Business travel, when approached with curiosity and awareness, can be a powerful lever for mindset development. It creates opportunities for empathy-building, perspective-shifting, and experiential learning. But to harness this potential, organizations must rethink both the why and how of professional mobility.

First, we must acknowledge the cognitive benefits of diverse environments. Research in organizational psychology and neuroscience shows that exposure to unfamiliar contexts enhances creativity, problem-solving, and cognitive flexibility. Teams that engage across cultures tend to approach challenges with more nuance and resilience.

Travel introduces productive friction, the kind that surfaces assumptions, invites new questions, and leads to innovation. But these benefits are not automatic. They require intentional design. Corporate travel should not be an afterthought or perk. It should be embedded within leadership development, onboarding, and team-building strategies. This might mean structured cultural exchange programs, immersive learning experiences in global markets, or reflective debriefs following international travel. Without integration, business travel remains surface-level and transactional. Ethics and sustainability must also be considered.

Corporate responsibility now extends beyond financial performance to include environmental stewardship and social impact. This means assessing the carbon cost of travel, favoring longer and more meaningful engagements over frequent short trips, and supporting sustainable vendors. It also means preparing employees to move through global contexts with humility, respect, and awareness of their organizational footprint. Professional mobility also intersects with issues of equity and access. Who gets to travel for work? Who benefits from global exposure? Too often, these opportunities are concentrated among senior leadership or particular departments. Inclusive mobility strategies can democratize professional travel by offering rotational programs, mentorship exchanges, and global learning platforms that benefit a wider range of employees.

In a post-geographic economy, cultural fluency becomes a core leadership skill. The ability to read a room, navigate difference, and adapt communication across borders is no longer optional. It is central to global relevance. Organizations that invest in developing this fluency through meaningful travel and cross-border engagement will be better positioned to thrive in complexity.

Technology plays a complementary role. While it cannot replace in-person connection, it can enhance travel experiences. Augmented reality, AI-powered translation, digital concierge tools, and immersive virtual training environments can prepare teams before they depart and help them stay connected after they return. Hybrid approaches to mobility, where in-person travel is supported by ongoing digital connection are shaping the future of professional exploration.

Corporate explorers benefit from taking time to reflect. Just as individuals reflect on personal travel, so too should professionals reflect on what they learn from their experiences abroad. What did they notice about communication styles? What insights emerged from cultural differences? What biases or assumptions were challenged? Structured reflection not only enhances learning but translates global experiences into actionable insight. In short, the organizations that will lead in the future are those that see travel not as an expense to manage but as an asset to cultivate.

Mobility is not just about movement; it's about mindset and mission alignment. In our final chapter, we turn to the long view of strategic foresight. How can we anticipate the future of travel? What trends are emerging? And what mindset will we need to navigate what comes next?

Here, mobility becomes a form of learning. The future-ready organization treats travel as a developmental space: a chance to break down silos and power dynamics, while expanding empathy, cultural intelligence, and perspective. When designed with intention, global movement cultivates leaders who listen deeply, adapt with humility, draw wisdom from difference and are ignited with the art of storytelling for impact. The ROI of corporate travel is not miles logged but minds expanded and teams that return transformed, capable of stewarding global futures with sensitivity and vision.

CONSIDERATIONS

# Travel in Times of Crisis

There are moments in history when movement itself becomes charged, politically, morally and emotionally. Pandemics, natural disasters, conflict, economic instability, social upheaval or crisis reshape not only where we can go, but how we go, and why.

In these periods, travel transforms. It becomes less about escape and more about responsibility. Less about leisure and more about awareness. It forces us to confront an essential truth: moving through the world is never separate from the world's condition.

Travel in times of crisis exposes the duality of mobility. It's freedom for some, impossibility for others. It reveals who has the privilege to leave, and who must stay. It underscores that mobility is not universal; it is structured by power, politics, and circumstance. Many travelers describe a deep shift after experiencing crisis firsthand or traveling during uncertain times. The mind becomes attuned not just to self-fulfillment, but to interdependence. The world's fragility becomes visible. Empathy expands. We recognize that travel is not personal, it's part of a shared ecosystem of resilience and risk.

Neuroscience tells us that uncertainty and disruption activate neural pathways associated with learning and adaptation. Crisis heightens awareness, but paired with reflection, it can deepen maturity. To move in a time of instability requires emotional regulation, humility, and ethical presence. It teaches us to read context sensitively, to honor collective grief, to soften our footprint, to act not just with curiosity, but with care.

Travel in times of crisis also changes pace. It becomes slower, more intentional, grounded in gratitude rather than entitlement. The traveler learns that movement is not guaranteed; it is borrowed

There is also the question of purpose. In crisis, travel becomes more overtly relational, about supporting others, reuniting with loved ones, reconnecting with community or land. For some, it becomes pilgrimage; for others, return. Movement turns inward as much as outward. Some journeys cannot be postponed: journeys to care, to witness, to serve, to heal. In such moments, travel becomes an act of commitment, not consumption. A declaration that connection still matters, even when the world constricts.

The conscious traveler must hold this tension:
To acknowledge privilege without paralysis.
To move, when necessary, stay when responsible, and understand the difference.
To recognize that every footprint during crisis carries weight, and every act of presence carries
consequence.

In crisis, travel teaches us resilience, but also restraint. It invites us to ask not only "Can I go?" but "Should I?", "Why?" and "How will I show up when I arrive?" It reminds us that movement is part of the social fabric, and in fragile times, fabric must be handled with care.

In the end, travel during a crisis is not defined by motion, but by meaning. It calls us to be ambassadors of steadiness, empathy, and contribution. It asks us to move through uncertainty not as spectators of global events, but as participants in shared humanity. Crisis does not close the possibility of travel. It deepens its purpose. In doing so, it transforms the traveler.

CONSIDERATIONS

# Where is travel going next?

As we near the end of this journey, one essential question remains: where is travel going next? If the previous chapters have explored the evolving why, how, and who of travel, this final chapter turns toward the horizon.

## MINDSET FOR THE FUTURE

In a world shaped by climate volatility, technological acceleration, cultural flux, and shifting values, the future of travel is being imagined, anticipated, and shaped. This is the role of strategic foresight, to explore the emerging signals of change, envision plausible futures, and develop the mindset to navigate what lies ahead.

Strategic foresight about where travel is going next is not prediction. It is a discipline rooted in systems thinking, scenario planning, and long-term visioning. It helps organizations, communities, and individuals prepare for uncertainty not by forecasting exact outcomes, but by mapping possibility. In the context of travel, foresight asks: What new patterns of movement are emerging? What global shifts will affect how, where, and why we travel? And how can we design systems that are both adaptive and principled?

Climate change remains the most urgent force reshaping the landscape of travel. Rising temperatures, extreme weather events, and sea-level rise will alter the physical viability of certain destinations and the ethics of accessing fragile environments. Travel infrastructure must become more resilient and responsive. Destinations will need

## CONSIDERATIONS

to grapple with managed tourism, ecological regeneration, and community protection.

The future of travel will demand greater responsibility from everyone involved, including solo and group travelers, industry leaders, governments, and the technologies that shape mobility. Technological transformation will also continue to redefine travel experiences. Artificial intelligence will personalize travel planning with increasing sophistication. Blockchain could enable secure, decentralized identity verification. Augmented and virtual reality will offer immersive previews (and perhaps full alternatives) to physical presence. But with these advances come ethical questions about data, equity, and authenticity. The role of technology in travel must be guided by values, not just convenience.

Cultural dynamics will shift as well. As nationalism and transnationalism continue to shape the geopolitical landscape, access to travel may become more uneven. The concept of global citizenship, rooted in shared responsibility and empathy, will be tested. Yet we may also see a resurgence in localized, rooted forms of exploration: slow travel, pilgrimage, ancestral journeys, and reciprocal exchanges that prioritize depth over novelty.

We must also prepare for behavioral and psychological shifts. Future travelers may prioritize mental health, solitude, or digital detox over entertainment and spectacle. Travel may increasingly be seen as a therapeutic modality, a space for healing, reflection, and reconnection with self and nature.

Neuroscience, psychology, and wellness science will play a growing role in shaping what we seek from movement. The business of travel will adapt accordingly. Industry leaders will need to anticipate future values like regeneration, equity, and emotional sustainability as central to their offerings. Emerging generations of travelers will expect transparency, social impact, and deep personalization. Companies that integrate foresight into their strategy will be better positioned to lead. Education and cultural institutions will also play a critical role.

As travel becomes more complex, preparing people to navigate difference, ambiguity, and disruption will be essential. Global fluency, ethical literacy, and critical thinking must be taught alongside traditional travel preparation. A mindset for the future is one that balances curiosity with discernment, ambition with responsibility and individual experience with a sense of global citizenship.

Ultimately, the future of travel is not fixed. It is a landscape of choices: technological, ecological, psychological, and relational. Strategic foresight gives us the tools to choose wisely. It reminds us that while we cannot control the future, we can shape it with the questions we ask, the systems we design, and the values we uphold.

This book began with a simple premise: that travel is changing, and that it can change us if we let it. We end with an invitation. As you move forward, whether across borders or in your own neighborhood, travel with intention and humility. Keep your mind on the move. Travel with a mindset that is ready and helps shape the future.

The horizon of travel will not be defined by depth, by how we move, what we notice, and who we become along the way. The most radical future of travel may not be faster, cheaper, or more automated, but more human. Choosing a pace that lets us understand where we are, taking the risks needed to build real connection, and making decisions that respect both place and people. In this future, travel is not just a way to see the world, but a way to learn how to belong to it.

## Considerations for Future-Ready Travel

To integrate the ideas in Part 5, consider:

- Travel with environmental awareness. Before booking, pause and ask: Is this distance worth the carbon? Consider slower routes, longer stays in fewer destinations, and offsetting as part of the planning, not the afterthought.
- Invest in meaningful circulation. Choose businesses that are locally owned, transparent, and regenerative. Let your money act as a vote for the world you want to move through.
- Practice cultural attunement. Learn five local phrases, understand one custom, and ask one question about history before arrival. Let humility be your welcome.
- Choose depth over density. Plan fewer stops and fuller immersion. Stay long enough to become a familiar face, not a passing consumer.
- See travel as exchange, not extraction. Before participating, ask: Am I taking a story or earning one? Seek relationships over

transactions and contribution over consumption.
- Model ethical mobility at work. Advocate for low-frequency/high-impact business travel, cultural immersion days, and post-trip reflection sharing within teams.
- Future-scan every journey. After each trip, note one emerging trend you witnessed, whether it's environmental, cultural, or technological, and consider how it shapes the future of travel and your role in it.

# Conclusion

Travel has always been more than movement. It is a reflection of who we are, how we think, and what we value. As the world accelerates (technologically, environmentally and socially) the need to pause, reflect, and reimagine the meaning of travel has never been more urgent.

This book has explored that meaning across many dimensions: the psychological roots of wanderlust, the neuroscience of experience, the evolution of travel identity, and the role of awe, discomfort, and attention in shaping the mind. We've examined the transformation of travel through digitalization, globalization, and shifting cultural norms, and what it takes to remain grounded as we move.

Throughout, one theme has emerged consistently: that travel is not simply a set of destinations, but a mindset. The future of travel will not be defined solely by the places we go, but by the

## CONCLUSION

presence we bring to those places. By our capacity to listen, to reflect, to adapt, and to grow.

The chapters on consideration, involving travelers, the travel industry, and corporate explorers, highlighted the systems-level shifts needed to make travel sustainable, inclusive, and meaningful. Yet those systemic shifts begin with individuals. With choices made before departure, during movement, and especially upon return. With the questions we ask, the relationships we form, and the stories we choose to tell.

Mindset for the future is not a fixed doctrine. It is a posture: curious, flexible, globally aware, and ethically rooted. It is about shifting from performance and consumption to presence and contribution. It means looking for genuine understanding instead of simply collecting experiences, and making sure our time in a place has meaning. It also calls for courage, the willingness to face uncertainty, question our assumptions, form relationships built on mutual respect, and take responsibility for how we show up in the world. The traveler of the future will be defined less by how far they go and more by how thoughtfully they engage with places, people, and themselves.

As you close this book, the journey doesn't end. Whether you're planning a trip, reflecting on past experiences, designing programs for others, or leading organizations into an interconnected world, we invite you to travel forward with intention. Carry with you the insights, practices, and questions offered here. Let them guide how you show up because travel is a mirror and a compass. It shows us who we are and helps us find who we're becoming.

And if travel teaches us anything, it is that belonging does not arise from arrival, but from attention. That meaning is made not by passing through places, but by allowing places to pass through us. That we are shaped not by how many borders we cross, but by how many internal (and external) boundaries we are willing to soften. In a world that's changing quickly, the priority isn't speed, it's depth. We need movement that's thoughtful, responsible, and future-minded.

# A Traveler's Toolkit - Practical Integration Guide

Insight only matters if it's applied. Experiences fade quickly without intentional follow-through, and growth requires repetition and structure.

This toolkit is not meant as a checklist, but as a set of habits you can use to make travel more meaningful and more responsible personally and professionally.

Effective travel unfolds in three stages: preparation, presence, and integration. Each stage asks for three things: curiosity, humility, and discipline. The following tools are designed to help you build those capacities in clear, practical steps.

# Before You Go: Preparing the Mindset

Travel begins with questions, not logistics.

Why am I going?
Who might this journey change me into?
What values will guide how I show up?

Pause before planning. Set a learning intention. Choose one theme to anchor your trip, whether it's attention, listening, humility, creativity, rest, connection.

Research what to do, and also how to behave. Learn greetings, gestures, etiquette. Understand the history beneath the scenery. Identify local voices and creators. Preparing well isn't about control; it's about readiness to be changed.

Pack a mental toolkit:

- A commitment to observe before interpreting.
- A willingness to be uncomfortable.
- The courage to ask, "What don't I understand yet?"

## CONCLUSION

**Neuroscience cue:**
Awe and anticipation activate the dopaminergic reward system, priming plasticity in the prefrontal cortex. Preparation is the neurochemical readiness for transformation.

# While You're There: Practicing Presence

Being present is a skill, and travel is one of the best ways to practice it. Use each day on the road to pay attention, slow down, and meet your surroundings with intention.

Move slower than you think you need to.
Sit longer than is comfortable.
Let silence teach you something.

Use curiosity as a compass. Ask open questions. Notice power dynamics. Look for local rhythms rather than tourist choreography. Participate, don't just witness. Contribute, don't merely consume.

Create rituals to anchor attention:

- A morning reflection before stepping outside
- A nightly note of what challenged you and what surprised you.
- A pause before taking a photo: "Am I seeing this, or collecting it?"

**Neuroscience cue:**
Novel environments stimulate the hippocampus and default-mode network. When paired with mindful

## CONCLUSION

presence, this increases neuroplasticity and emotional regulation, turning moments into meaning.

# Coming Home: Integrating the Experience

The most important part of travel often happens after the return. Not every journey transforms us, nor should it. What matters is noticing what each experience brings, and choosing what, if anything, we want to carry forward.

Integration requires slowing down the re-entry. Protect time for reflection before routine rushes back in. Write, voice note, or speak your experience aloud. Capture the questions that come to mind.

Ask yourself:

- What new perspective did I gain?
- What belief did I release?
- What did this place teach me about belonging, care, and self?

Decide on one thing you want to carry forward from the trip and weave it into your daily life. It might be a small habit, a shift in perspective, or a new way of relating to others. What matters is choosing something manageable and letting it shape your routine in a realistic way. The goal is not to create a travel version of yourself and a home version of yourself, but to let the two converge.

**Neuroscience cue:**
Integration consolidates memory through the hippocampus and medial prefrontal cortex. Reflection literally stabilizes growth at the neural level.

# A Philosophy of Everyday Travel

The final practice is learning to bring a traveler's mindset into daily life. It means paying closer attention to familiar spaces, noticing details you usually pass by, and approaching routine interactions with curiosity.

Treat your neighborhood as a place still worth exploring. Let everyday moments prompt questions, reflection, and connection. This approach strengthens awareness, adaptability, and cultural openness. These are skills that matter just as much at home as they do abroad.

We hope this toolkit was helpful in offering guidance for developing these habits in a consistent, grounded way.

It should encourage you to:

- Approach experiences with curiosity rather than performance.
- Bring home insights that influence how you think and act, not just memories
- Apply what you've learned in ways that improve how you show up in daily life and relationships.

## CONCLUSION

Travel can spark change, but lasting growth comes from the choices you make afterward. Integration is the real work, and it continues long after the suitcase is unpacked.

# References

- Adams, W. M. (2006). "The future of sustainability: Re-thinking environment and development." IUCN Report.

- Ahuvia, A. C. (2005). "Beyond the extended self: Loved objects and consumers' identity narratives." Journal of Consumer Research, 32(1), 171–184.

- Amichai-Hamburger, Y., & Hayat, Z. (2011). "The impact of the Internet on the social lives of users: A representative sample from 13 countries." Computers in Human Behavior, 27(1), 585–589.

- Argyris, C. (1991). "Teaching smart people how to learn." Harvard Business Review, 69(3), 99–109.

- Arnsten, A. F. (2009). "Stress signalling pathways that impair prefrontal cortex structure and function." Nature Reviews Neuroscience, 10(6), 410–422.

- Aronson, E. (2008). The Social Animal. Worth Publishers.

- Baker, S. C., & Kim, H. Y. (2020). "The psychology of re-entry: Emotional and cognitive adaptation after travel." Journal of Cross-Cultural Psychology, 51(4), 256–274.

## REFERENCES

- Bandura, A. (1977). Social Learning Theory. Prentice-Hall.

- Bartlett, F. C. (1932). Remembering: A Study in Experimental and Social Psychology. Cambridge University Press.

- Bateson, G. (1972). Steps to an Ecology of Mind. University of Chicago Press.

- Baum, T., & Hai, N. T. (2020). "Hospitality, tourism, human rights and the impact of COVID-19." International Journal of Contemporary Hospitality Management, 32(7), 2397–2407.

- Baumeister, R. F. (1998). "The self." In D. T. Gilbert, S. T. Fiske, & G. Lindzey (Eds.), The Handbook of Social Psychology. McGraw-Hill.

- Baumeister, R. F., & Leary, M. R. (1995). "The need to belong: Desire for interpersonal attachments as a fundamental human motivation." Psychological Bulletin, 117(3), 497–529.

- Baumeister, R. F., & Vohs, K. D. (2007). "Self-regulation, ego depletion, and motivation." Social and Personality Psychology Compass, 1(1), 115–128.

- Benedek, M., & Kaernbach, C. (2011). "Physiological correlates and emotional specificity of human awe." Biological Psychology, 86(3), 337–345.

- Berger, P. L., & Luckmann, T. (1966). The Social Construction of Reality. Anchor Books.

- Berkes, F. (2009). "Evolution of co-management: Role of knowledge generation, bridging organizations and social learning." Journal of Environmental Management, 90(5), 1692–1702.

- Berry, J. W. (1997). "Immigration, acculturation, and adaptation." Applied Psychology, 46(1), 5–34.

- Bhaskar, R. (1998). The Possibility of Naturalism. Routledge.

- Bishop, S. R., et al. (2004). "Mindfulness: A proposed operational definition." Clinical Psychology: Science and Practice, 11(3), 230–241.

- Biss, R. K., & Hasher, L. (2011). "Delighted and distracted: Positive affect increases distractibility in older adults." Emotion, 11(4), 776–781.

- Bohm, D. (1996). On Dialogue. Routledge.

- Bosker, B. (2016). Future Presence: How Virtual Reality Is Changing Human Connection, Intimacy, and the Limits of Ordinary Life. Houghton Mifflin Harcourt.

- Bowlby, J. (1969). Attachment and Loss: Vol. 1. Attachment. Basic Books.

- Bramwell, B., & Lane, B. (2011). "Critical research on the governance of tourism and sustainability." Journal of Sustainable Tourism, 19(4–5), 411–421.

## REFERENCES

- Bronfenbrenner, U. (1979). The Ecology of Human Development: Experiments by Nature and Design. Harvard University Press.

- Brown, L. (2009). "The transformative power of the international sojourn: An ethnographic study of the international student experience." Annals of Tourism Research, 36(3), 502–521.

- Buber, M. (1970). I and Thou. Charles Scribner's Sons.

- Butler, J. (2005). Giving an Account of Oneself. Fordham University Press.

- Cacioppo, J. T., & Patrick, W. (2008). Loneliness: Human Nature and the Need for Social Connection. W. W. Norton.

- Caligiuri, P., & Bonache, J. (2016). "Evolving and enduring challenges in global mobility." Journal of World Business, 51(1), 127–141.

- Carpenter, S. R., et al. (2009). "Resilience: Accounting for the noncomputable." Proceedings of the National Academy of Sciences, 106(36), 15160–15161.

- Carr, A. (2020). "Digital mobility and identity." Journal of Travel Research, 59(8), 1390–1401.

- Carr, A. (2020). "Digital nomads: Work, lifestyle, and the new mobility." Journal of Management & Organization, 26(2), 236–251.

- Carr, N. (2010). The Shallows: What the Internet Is Doing to Our Brains. W. W. Norton.

- Carrigan, M., & Attalla, A. (2001). "The myth of the ethical consumer." Journal of Consumer Marketing, 18(7), 560–578.

- Cassidy, J. (1999). "The nature of the child's ties." In Handbook of Attachment. Guilford Press.

- Cohen, E. (1972). "Toward a sociology of international tourism." Social Research, 39(1), 164–182.

- Cohen, E. (1979). "A phenomenology of tourist experiences." Sociology, 13(2), 179–201.

- Collings, D. G., et al. (2019). "Global mobility in a disruptive world." Journal of World Business, 54(4), 247–257.

- Cooper, A., & Johnson, R. (2019). "Regenerative tourism: A new paradigm for a rapidly changing world." Tourism Recreation Research, 44(3), 368–379.

- Creswell, J. W. (2013). Qualitative Inquiry and Research Design: Choosing Among Five Approaches. Sage Publications.

- Csikszentmihalyi, M. (1990). Flow: The Psychology of Optimal Experience. Harper & Row.

# REFERENCES

- Damasio, A. (1999). The Feeling of What Happens: Body and Emotion in the Making of Consciousness. Harcourt.

- Darwall, S. (2006). The Second-Person Standpoint: Morality, Respect, and Accountability. Harvard University Press.

- Deci, E. L., & Ryan, R. M. (2000). "The 'what' and 'why' of goal pursuits: Human needs and self-determination." Psychological Inquiry, 11(4), 227–268.

- Dennett, D. (1991). Consciousness Explained. Little, Brown.

- Dervin, B. (1998). "Sense-making theory revisited." In International Communications Association Proceedings.

- Dewey, J. (1934). Art as Experience. Perigee Books.

- Digital Nomadism Research Group. (2021). "Global mobility, remote work, and the rise of nomadic labor." International Journal of Sociology and Social Policy, 41(9/10), 1175–1193.

- DuBois, D. (2017). "Tourism and inequality: Emerging issues and global challenges." Tourism Geographies, 19(4), 587–590.

- Dwivedi, Y., Johnson, S., & Fuchs, C. (2022). "Awe and well-being: The restorative effects of novelty." Emotion Review, 14(2), 128–141.

- Dwyer, L., & Thomas, F. (2023). "Regenerative tourism: Beyond sustainability." Journal of Sustainable Tourism, 31(2), 205–223.

- Edwards, A. (2010). Being an Expert Professional Practitioner. Springer.

- Ekman, P., & Friesen, W. V. (1975). Unmasking the Face. Prentice-Hall.

- Elkington, J. (1997). Cannibals with Forks: The Triple Bottom Line of 21st Century Business. Capstone.

- Ellsworth, P. C., & Scherer, K. R. (2003). "Appraisal processes in emotion." In Handbook of Affective Sciences, Oxford University Press.

- Epel, E. S., et al. (2013). "Awe and prosocial behavior." Journal of Personality and Social Psychology, 105(2), 225–238.

- Faulkner, B. (2001). "Towards a framework for tourism disaster management." Tourism Management, 22(2), 135–147.

- Ferrell, O. C., & Fraedrich, J. (2015). Business Ethics: Ethical Decision Making and Cases. Cengage Learning.

- Festinger, L. (1957). A Theory of Cognitive Dissonance. Stanford University Press.

- Florida, R. (2012). The Rise of the Creative Class—Revisited. Basic Books.

## REFERENCES

- Frankl, V. E. (1959). Man's Search for Meaning. Beacon Press.

- Fredrickson, B. L. (2001). "The broaden-and-build theory of positive emotions." American Psychologist, 56(3), 218–226.

- Friedman, T. L. (2005). The World Is Flat. Farrar, Straus and Giroux.

- Fullagar, S., Wilson, E., & Markwell, K. (2012). Slow Tourism: Experiences and Mobilities. Channel View.

- Gable, S. L., & Haidt, J. (2005). "What (and why) is positive psychology?" Review of General Psychology, 9(2), 103–110.

- Gazzaley, A., & Rosen, L. (2016). The Distracted Mind: Ancient Brains in a High-Tech World. MIT Press.

- Giddens, A. (1991). Modernity and Self-Identity: Self and Society in the Late Modern Age. Stanford University Press.

- Gioda, N., & McAdams, D. P. (2020). "Narrative identity development across contexts." Personality and Social Psychology Review, 24(3), 201–223.

- Gioia, D. A., & Manz, C. C. (1985). "Linking cognition and behavior: A script processing interpretation of vicarious learning." Academy of Management Review, 10(3), 527–539.

- Giorgi, G. (2012). "Liminality and transformation: The psychology of threshold experiences." Journal of Humanistic Psychology, 52(4), 414–431.

- Gladwell, M. (2005). Blink: The Power of Thinking Without Thinking. Little, Brown.

- Goffman, E. (1959). The Presentation of Self in Everyday Life. Anchor Books.

- Goleman, D. (2006). Social Intelligence: The New Science of Human Relationships. Bantam.

- Gössling, S., & Higham, J. (2021). "The shift to low-carbon mobility." Journal of Sustainable Tourism, 29(2–3), 353–374.

- Gössling, S., Scott, D., & Hall, C. M. (2015). "Tourism and water." Tourism Management, 50, 1–15.

- Grant, A. (2013). Give and Take: A Revolutionary Approach to Success. Viking.

- Gratton, L., & Scott, A. (2016). The 100-Year Life: Living and Working in an Age of Longevity. Bloomsbury.

- Gretzel, U., Sigala, M., Xiang, Z., & Koo, C. (2015). "Smart tourism: Foundations and developments." Electronic Markets, 25(3), 179–188.

## REFERENCES

- Grice, H. P. (1975). "Logic and conversation." In Syntax and Semantics, Vol. 3: Speech Acts. Academic Press.

- Haidt, J. (2000). "The positive moral emotion of elevation." Review of General Psychology, 4(3), 304–314.

- Haidt, J., & Keltner, D. (2004). "Appreciation of beauty and excellence." In Character Strengths and Virtues. Oxford University Press.

- Hall, C. M. (2011). "Policy learning and policy failure in sustainable tourism governance." Journal of Sustainable Tourism, 19(4–5), 649–671.

- Han, H., & Hyun, S. S. (2018). "Role of motivations for travel: Tourism experience and well-being." Journal of Travel Research, 57(5), 612–626.

- Hargie, O. (2011). Skilled Interpersonal Communication: Research, Theory and Practice. Routledge.

- Heath, C., & Heath, D. (2010). Switch: How to Change Things When Change Is Hard. Broadway Books.

- Heifetz, R., Grashow, A., & Linsky, M. (2009). The Practice of Adaptive Leadership. Harvard Business Press.

- Henderson, J. C. (2007). "Tourism crises: Causes, consequences and management." Butterworth-Heinemann.

- Hermans, H. J. (2001). "The dialogical self: Toward a theory of personal and cultural positioning." Culture & Psychology, 7(3), 243–281.

- Hobfoll, S. E. (1989). "Conservation of resources: A new attempt at conceptualizing stress." American Psychologist, 44(3), 513–524.

- Hofstede, G. (2001). Culture's Consequences: Comparing Values, Behaviors, Institutions and Organizations Across Nations. Sage Publications.

- Holbrook, M. B., & Hirschman, E. C. (1982). "The experiential aspects of consumption: Consumer fantasies, feelings, and fun." Journal of Consumer Research, 9(2), 132–140.

- Holling, C. S. (1973). "Resilience and stability of ecological systems." Annual Review of Ecology and Systematics, 4, 1–23.

- Immordino-Yang, M. H., & Damasio, A. (2007). "We feel, therefore we learn." Mind, Brain, and Education, 1(1), 3–10.

- Inkson, K., & Myers, B. A. (2003). "The psychological contract and global mobility." International Journal of Human Resource Management, 14(3), 517–533.

# REFERENCES

- IPCC. (2021). Climate Change 2021: The Physical Science Basis. Cambridge University Press.

- Jackendoff, R. (2007). Language, Consciousness, Culture. MIT Press.

- Jamal, T., & Camargo, B. A. (2014). "Sustainable tourism, justice and an ethic of care." Tourism Recreation Research, 39(1), 9–28.

- Jenkins, R. (2008). Social Identity. Routledge.

- Jopp, R., & Mair, J. (2012). "Crisis preparedness in the tourism industry." Journal of Travel & Tourism Marketing, 29(1), 1–15.

- Kabat-Zinn, J. (1994). Wherever You Go, There You Are. Hyperion.

- Kahneman, D. (2011). Thinking, Fast and Slow. Farrar, Straus and Giroux.

- Kaplan, S. (1995). "The restorative benefits of nature: Toward an integrative framework." Journal of Environmental Psychology, 15(3), 169–182.

- Kauffman, S. (1996). At Home in the Universe: The Search for the Laws of Self-Organization. Oxford University Press.

- Kelly, G. A. (1955). The Psychology of Personal Constructs. Routledge.

- Keltner, D., & Haidt, J. (2003). "Approaching awe, a moral, spiritual, and aesthetic emotion." Cognition and Emotion, 17(2), 297–314.

- Kennedy, E. B., & Dornan, M. (2020). "Climate change and tourism adaptation." Tourism Management, 81, 104162.

- Kiesa, A., & Narayan, J. (2016). "Global citizenship education: Renewal and resilience." International Journal of Development Education and Global Learning, 8(2), 87–100.

- Kohonen, I. (2005). "Developing global leaders through international assignments: An identity construction perspective." Personnel Review, 34(1), 22–36.

- Kounios, J., & Beeman, M. (2015). The Eureka Factor: Aha Moments, Creative Insight, and the Brain. Random House.

- Kraus, M., & Stephens, N. M. (2012). "A cultural psychology perspective on social class." Current Directions in Psychological Science, 21(6), 343–348.

- Kross, E., & Ayduk, Ö. (2011). "Self-distancing: Theory, research, and current directions." Social and Personality Psychology Compass, 5(8), 631–645.

- Landau, M. J., Greenberg, J., & Solomon, S. (2008). "A sign of the times: The psychology of cultural worldviews." Social and Personality Psychology Compass, 2(3), 1135–1152.

- Langer, E. J. (1989). Mindfulness. Addison-Wesley.

- Langer, E. J. (2009). Counterclockwise: Mindful Health and the Psychology of Possibility. Ballantine Books.

- LeDoux, J. (1996). The Emotional Brain: The Mysterious Underpinnings of Emotional Life. Simon & Schuster.

- Lee, J., & Kim, H. (2020). "Digital nomads, mobility, and the psychological effects of rootlessness." Journal of Travel Research, 59(8), 1402–1416.

- Lewin, K. (1951). Field Theory in Social Science. Harper & Row.

- Lidwell, W., Holden, K., & Butler, J. (2010). Universal Principles of Design. Rockport.

- Line, N., & Hanks, L. (2019). "Sustainable tourism strategies for the future." Journal of Hospitality Marketing & Management, 28(8), 1–19.

- Linguistic Relativity Hypothesis: Whorf, B. L. (1956). Language, Thought, and Reality: Selected Writings of Benjamin Lee Whorf. MIT Press.

- Lipman, G., & Vorster, S. (2018). "The dawn of regenerative tourism." EarthCheck Institute Report.

- Lisle, D. (2006). The Global Politics of Contemporary Travel Writing. Cambridge University Press.

- Lonergan, B. J. (1972). Method in Theology. Herder and Herder.

- Lupien, S. J., et al. (2009). "Effects of stress throughout the lifespan on the brain, behaviour, and cognition." Nature Reviews Neuroscience, 10(6), 434–445.

- MacCannell, D. (1976). The Tourist: A New Theory of the Leisure Class. University of California Press.

- Maguire, E. A., et al. (2000). "Navigation-related structural change in the hippocampi of taxi drivers." Proceedings of the National Academy of Sciences, 97(8), 4398–4403.

- Margolis, J. D., & Walsh, J. P. (2003). "Misery loves companies: Rethinking social initiatives by business." Administrative Science Quarterly, 48(2), 268–305.

- Markus, H., & Kitayama, S. (1991). "Culture and self: Implications for cognition, emotion, and motivation." Psychological Review, 98(2), 224–253.

- Markus, H., & Nurius, P. (1986). "Possible selves." American Psychologist, 41(9), 954–969.

# REFERENCES

- Maslow, A. H. (1943). "A theory of human motivation." Psychological Review, 50(4), 370–396.

- Maslow, A. H. (1962). Toward a Psychology of Being. Van Nostrand.

- McAdams, D. P. (2001). "The psychology of life stories." Review of General Psychology, 5(2), 100–122.

- McAdams, D. P., & McLean, K. C. (2013). "Narrative identity." Current Directions in Psychological Science, 22(3), 233–238.

- McEwen, B. S., & Wingfield, J. C. (2010). "What is stress? Integrating the concept of stress with physiology." Integrative and Comparative Biology, 50(3), 494–508.

- Meadows, D. H. (2008). Thinking in Systems: A Primer. Chelsea Green Publishing.

- Merrilees, B., Miller, D., & Herington, C. (2012). "Sustainability and stakeholder management in tourism." Tourism Management, 33(2), 307–316.

- Mesquita, B., & Leu, J. (2007). "The cultural psychology of emotion." In Handbook of Cultural Psychology.

- Mezirow, J. (1997). "Transformative learning: Theory to practice." New Directions for Adult and Continuing Education, 74, 5–12.

- Miller, D. (2010). Stuff. Polity Press.

- Mittelman, J. H. (2000). The Globalization Syndrome. Princeton University Press.

- Naidoo, P., & Sharpley, R. (2018). "Local perceptions of the impacts of tourism." Journal of Sustainable Tourism, 26(3), 316–332.

- Neal, J. D., & Gursoy, D. (2008). "A multifaceted analysis of tourism satisfaction." Tourism Management, 29(1), 84–95.

- Neff, K. (2011). Self-Compassion: The Proven Power of Being Kind to Yourself. HarperCollins.

- Nicolescu, B. (2002). Manifesto of Transdisciplinarity. SUNY Press.

- Niemeyer, R. A. (2000). "Meaning reconstruction in the wake of loss." Death Studies, 24(6), 541–558.

- Norman, D. (2013). The Design of Everyday Things. MIT Press.

- Noy, C. (2004). "This trip really changed me: Backpackers' narratives of self-change." Annals of Tourism Research, 31(1), 78–102.

- O'Reilly, K. (2006). International Migration and Social Theory. Palgrave.

- O'Toole, J., Galbraith, J., & Lawler, E. E. (2002). The New American Workplace. Palgrave.

- Pariser, E. (2011). The Filter Bubble: What the Internet Is Hiding from You. Penguin Press.

## REFERENCES

- Pearce, D. G., & Schott, C. (2005). "Tourism distribution channels: Practices and performance." International Journal of Tourism Research, 7(2), 95–111.

- Pearce, P. L., & Lee, U. (2005). "Developing the travel career approach to tourist motivation." Journal of Travel Research, 43(3), 226–237.

- Pennebaker, J. W. (1997). "Writing about emotional experiences as a therapeutic process." Psychological Science, 8(3), 162–166.

- Peters, A., McEwen, B. S., & Friston, K. (2017). "Uncertainty and stress: Why it causes disease and how it is mastered." Progress in Neurobiology, 156, 164–188.

- Pine, B. J., & Gilmore, J. H. (1999). The Experience Economy. Harvard Business School Press.

- Pinker, S. (1994). The Language Instinct. William Morrow.

- Place Attachment Theory: Scannell, L., & Gifford, R. (2010). "Defining place attachment: A tripartite organizing framework." Journal of Environmental Psychology, 30(1), 1–10.

- Porges, S. W. (2011). The Polyvagal Theory: Neurophysiological Foundations of Emotions, Attachment, Communication, and Self-Regulation. Norton.

- Porter, M. E., & Kramer, M. R. (2011). "Creating shared value." Harvard Business Review, 89(1–2), 62–77. • Prebensen, N. K., Chen, J. S., & Uysal, M. (Eds.). (2014). Creating Experience Value in Tourism. CABI.

- Posner, M. I., & Rothbart, M. K. (2007). Educating the Human Brain. APA.

- Prensky, M. (2010). "Digital wisdom: Hope to make us all wiser." Innovate: Journal of Online Education, 5(3).

- Ricoeur, P. (1984). Time and Narrative. University of Chicago Press.

- Ricœur, P. (1991). From Text to Action. Northwestern University Press.

- Ritchie, B. W. (2004). "Chaos, crises and disasters: A strategic approach to crisis management in the tourism industry." Tourism Management, 25(6), 669–683.

- Rogers, C. R. (1957). "The necessary and sufficient conditions of therapeutic personality change." Journal of Consulting Psychology, 21(2), 95–103.

- Rosenberg, M. B. (2003). Nonviolent Communication: A Language of Life. PuddleDancer Press.

## REFERENCES

- Scannell, L., & Gifford, R. (2010). "Defining place attachment: A tripartite framework." Journal of Environmental Psychology, 30(1), 1–10.

- Scharmer, O. (2009). Theory U: Leading from the Future as It Emerges. Berrett-Koehler.

- Schwartz, B. (2004). The Paradox of Choice: Why More Is Less. HarperCollins.

- Seligman, M. E. P. (2011). Flourish: A Visionary New Understanding of Happiness and Well-Being. Free Press.

- Senge, P. M. (1990). The Fifth Discipline. Doubleday.

- Sharpley, R. (2009). Tourism Development and the Environment. Earthscan.

- Sheller, M., & Urry, J. (2006). "The new mobilities paradigm." Environment and Planning A, 38(2), 207–226.

- Siegal, D. J. (2012). The Developing Mind: How Relationships and the Brain Interact to Shape Who We Are. Guilford Press.

- Slaughter, R. (2004). Futures Beyond Dystopia. Routledge.

- Smallwood, J., & Schooler, J. W. (2015). "The science of mind wandering: Empirically navigating the stream of consciousness." Annual Review of Psychology, 66, 487–518.

- Smith, J. A., & Eatough, V. (2007). "Interpretative phenomenological analysis." In Qualitative Psychology. Sage Publications.

- Smith, L. T. (1999). Decolonizing Methodologies: Research and Indigenous Peoples. Zed Books.

- Smith, S. M., & Vela, E. (2001). "Environmental context-dependent memory: A review and meta-analysis." Psychonomic Bulletin & Review, 8(2), 203–220.

- Spitzberg, B. H., & Changnon, G. (2009). "Conceptualizing intercultural competence." In The SAGE Handbook of Intercultural Competence. Sage Publications.

- Squire, L. R. (1992). "Memory and the hippocampus." Psychological Review, 99(2), 195–231.

- Staw, B. M., Sandelands, L. E., & Dutton, J. E. (1981). "Threat rigidity effects in organizational behavior." Administrative Science Quarterly, 26(4), 501–524.

- Steffen, W., et al. (2015). "Planetary boundaries: Guiding human development on a changing planet." Science, 347(6223), 1259855.

- Steiner, C. J., & Reisinger, Y. (2006). "Understanding existential authenticity." Annals of Tourism Research, 33(2), 299–318.

## REFERENCES

- Stets, J. E., & Burke, P. J. (2000). "Identity theory and social identity theory." Social Psychology Quarterly, 63(3), 224–237.

- Stewart, E. J., & Mallon, K. (2020). "Tourism, mindfulness, and well-being." Annals of Tourism Research, 83, 102934.

- Stiglitz, J. E. (2002). Globalization and Its Discontents. W. W. Norton.

- Stoner, J. A. F. (2013). "What does sustainability mean for business?" Journal of Management Education, 37(3), 389–393.

- Tajfel, H., & Turner, J. C. (1979). "An integrative theory of intergroup conflict." In The Social Psychology of Intergroup Relations. Brooks/Cole.

- Taylor, S. E. (1989). Positive Illusions. Basic Books.

- Ting-Toomey, S. (1999). Communicating Across Cultures. Guilford Press.

- Tuan, Y.-F. (1977). Space and Place: The Perspective of Experience. University of Minnesota Press.

- Turner, V. (1969). The Ritual Process: Structure and Anti-Structure. Aldine.

- Tversky, A., & Kahneman, D. (1974). "Judgment under uncertainty: Heuristics and biases." Science, 185(4157), 1124–1131.

- Tversky, B., & Hard, B. M. (2009). "Embodied and disembodied cognition: Spatial perspective-taking." Cognition, 110(1), 124–129.

- Ulrich, R. S. (1984). "View through a window may influence recovery from surgery." Science, 224(4647), 420–421.

- United Nations World Tourism Organization (UNWTO). (2019). Tourism for Sustainable Development Report.

- Urry, J. (2002). The Tourist Gaze. Sage Publications.

- Van Gennep, A. (1909). The Rites of Passage. University of Chicago Press (1960 translation).

- Van Manen, M. (1990). Researching Lived Experience. SUNY Press.

- Visser, W. (2011). The Age of Responsibility: CSR 2.0. Wiley.

- Watkins, M. (2000). Invisible Guests: The Development of Imaginal Dialogues. Spring Publications.

- Wegner, D. M. (1987). "Transactive memory: A contemporary analysis of the group mind." In Theories of Group Behavior. Springer.

- White, R. W. (1959). "Motivation reconsidered: The concept of competence." Psychological Review, 66(5), 297–333.

# REFERENCES

- Whiten, A., & Erdal, D. (2012). "The human socio-cognitive niche." Current Anthropology, 53(6), 719–746.

- Wilkerson, M. (2019). "Ethical mobility and global citizenship." Global Studies Journal, 12(4), 1–16.

- Williams, A. M., & Hall, C. M. (2002). "Tourism, migration, and global change." Tourism Geographies, 4(1), 5–27.

- Wood, A. M., & Tarrier, N. (2010). "Positive clinical psychology." The Clinical Psychologist, 14(1), 10–12.

- World Economic Forum. (2020). The Future of Travel & Tourism: Scenarios to 2030.

- Yaden, D. B., Haidt, J., et al. (2017). "The varieties of self-transcendent experience." Review of General Psychology, 21(2), 143–160.

- Yarnal, C. M., & Chick, G. (2010). "Serious leisure and place attachment in shared travel experiences." Leisure Sciences, 32(3), 233–255.

- Yeoman, I. (2012). 2050: Tomorrow's Tourism. Channel View Publications.

- Zajonc, R. B. (1980). "Feeling and thinking: Preferences need no inferences." American Psychologist, 35(2), 151–175.

- Zimmerman, B. J., & Schunk, D. H. (2011). Handbook of Self-Regulation of Learning and Performance. Routledge.

www.ingramcontent.com/pod-product-compliance
Lightning Source LLC
Chambersburg PA
CBHW050556170426
43201CB00011B/1715